CHE

CHE

A GRAPHIC BIOGRAPHY

SID JACOBSON AND ERNIE COLÓN

A NOVEL GRAPHIC FROM HILL AND WANG

A DIVISION OF FARRAR, STRAUS AND GIROUX   NEW YORK

HILL AND WANG
A DIVISION OF FARRAR, STRAUS AND GIROUX
18 WEST 18TH STREET, NEW YORK 10011

TEXT COPYRIGHT © 2009 BY SID JACOBSON
ARTWORK COPYRIGHT © 2009 BY ERNESTO COLÓN
ALL RIGHTS RESERVED
DISTRIBUTED IN CANADA BY D&M PUBLISHERS, INC.
PRINTED IN THE UNITED STATES OF AMERICA
FIRST EDITION, 2009

LIBRARY OF CONGRESS CATALOGING-IN-PUBLICATION DATA
JACOBSON, SIDNEY.
    CHE : A GRAPHIC BIOGRAPHY / SID JACOBSON AND ERNIE COLÓN. -- 1ST ED.
        P. CM.
    "A NOVEL GRAPHIC FROM HILL AND WANG."
    ISBN-13: 978-0-8090-9492-9 (HARDCOVER : ALK. PAPER)
    ISBN-10: 0-8090-9492-4 (HARDCOVER : ALK. PAPER)
    1. GUEVARA, ERNESTO, 1928-1967. 2. GUEVARA, ERNESTO, 1928-1967--PICTORIAL WORKS.
    3. GUERRILLAS--LATIN AMERICA--BIOGRAPHY. 4. GUERRILLAS--LATIN AMERICA--PICTORIAL WORKS.
    I. COLÓN, ERNIE. II. TITLE.

F2849.22.G85J27 2009
980.03'5--DC22

2009004410

WWW.FSGBOOKS.COM

1 3 5 7 9 10 8 6 4 2

WE DEDICATE THIS BOOK TO OUR WIVES,

RUTH ASHBY COLÓN AND SHURE JACOBSON,

WHO WERE ALWAYS THERE TO SHARE THE WORST AND ENJOY THE BEST

CONTENTS

CHE

YOU THINK LA PODEROSA CAN HANDLE A LONG JOURNEY, ALBERTO?

FOR YOU, MY LOVESICK PUPPY, IT WILL GO TO THE MOON!

CHAPTER 1:
THE MOTORCYCLE DIARIST

ON JANUARY 4, 1952, ERNESTO GUEVARA DE LA SERNA, A TALL, HOLLYWOOD-HANDSOME MEDICAL STUDENT, STILL TWO YEARS SHORT OF HIS DEGREE, CLIMBED ONTO THE BACK OF HIS BEST FRIEND'S BATTERED NORTON MOTORCYCLE AND THE TWO WENT OFF FOR A RIDE.

THE EXPEDITION THE TWO EMBARKED ON WOULD LAST MORE THAN SIX MONTHS. WHAT'S MORE, IT WOULD LAUNCH THE YOUNG MEDICAL STUDENT ON A MUCH LONGER, LIFE- AND WORLD-CHANGING JOURNEY.

3

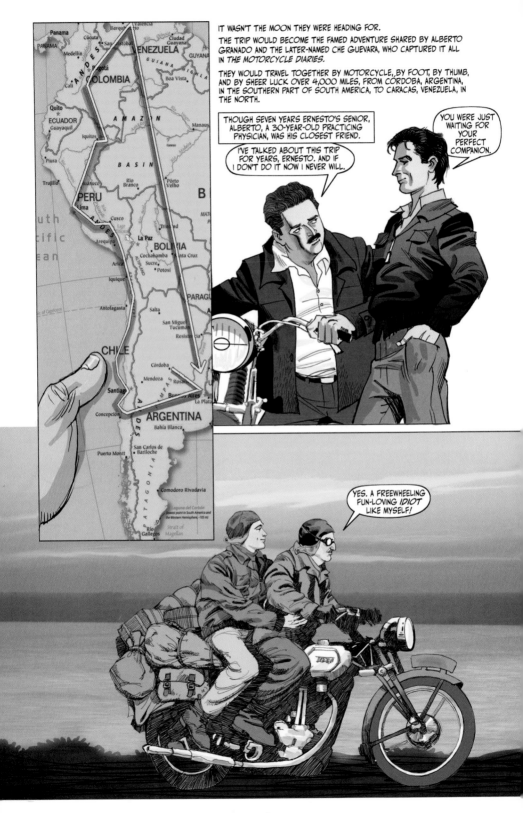

IT WASN'T THE MOON THEY WERE HEADING FOR.

THE TRIP WOULD BECOME THE FAMED ADVENTURE SHARED BY ALBERTO GRANADO AND THE LATER-NAMED CHE GUEVARA, WHO CAPTURED IT ALL IN *THE MOTORCYCLE DIARIES*.

THEY WOULD TRAVEL TOGETHER BY MOTORCYCLE, BY FOOT, BY THUMB, AND BY SHEER LUCK OVER 4,000 MILES, FROM CÓRDOBA, ARGENTINA, IN THE SOUTHERN PART OF SOUTH AMERICA, TO CARACAS, VENEZUELA, IN THE NORTH.

THOUGH SEVEN YEARS ERNESTO'S SENIOR, ALBERTO, A 30-YEAR-OLD PRACTICING PHYSICIAN, WAS HIS CLOSEST FRIEND.

I'VE TALKED ABOUT THIS TRIP FOR YEARS, ERNESTO. AND IF I DON'T DO IT NOW I NEVER WILL.

YOU WERE JUST WAITING FOR YOUR PERFECT COMPANION.

YES. A FREEWHEELING FUN-LOVING *IDIOT* LIKE MYSELF!

ALBERTO HAD BEEN RIGHT: HIS COMPANION WAS A LOVESICK PUPPY. THEIR FIRST STOP WAS THE ATLANTIC COAST OF MIRAMAR, WHERE ERNESTO WISHED TO SEE HIS GREAT LOVE AND PRESENT HER WITH A PUPPY OF HER OWN.

I HAD TO SEE YOU, MY LOVE.

CHICHINA FERREYRA WAS A BEAUTIFUL 16-YEAR-OLD HEIRESS OF ENORMOUS WEALTH, WHOM ERNESTO DESIRED TO MARRY...

HE HAD BROUGHT CHICHINA THE DOG AS A TOKEN OF HIS LOVE, AND HE ASKED HER FOR...

YOUR *BRACELET*. CAN I TAKE IT TO GUIDE ME AND REMIND ME OF YOUR LOVE?

SHE DID *NOT* GIVE IT TO HIM.

AND THOUGH HIS EXPECTED TWO-DAY STAY WITH HER "STRETCHED LIKE RUBBER INTO EIGHT," HE KNEW WHEN HE LEFT...

SHE WISHES ME WELL... SHE GIVES ME MONEY TO BUY A SCARF... BUT I'M AFRAID IT IS OVER.

BUT HE WOULD NOT *COMPLETELY* GIVE UP HOPE. INSTEAD, HE EMBRACED THE JOURNEY, WHICH HAD ITS UPS...

...AND ITS DOWNS!

AAAAA

WATCH IT, ALBERTO! YOU'RE *LOSING* CONTROL!

5

CERTAINLY, ERNESTO HAD LOST SOME OF HIS EARLIER CAUTION. JUST TWO YEARS BEFORE, ON AN EARLIER MOTORIZED BIKE TRIP THROUGH ARGENTINA...

COME WITH ME, ERNESTO. I'LL PULL YOU ON THIS ROPE AND YOU'LL GET THERE FASTER.

THANKS, BUT NO. I'LL TAKE THE SLOWER AND *SAFER* ROUTE.

IT PROVED SAFER INDEED.

THAT'S MY FRIEND'S MOTORCYCLE.

THEN YOU HAVE OUR SYMPATHY. YOUR FRIEND DID NOT SURVIVE THE ACCIDENT.

THEN, HE HAD, TRAVELED TO THE JOSE J. PUENTE LEPROSARIUM TO WORK ALONGSIDE ALBERTO, WHO WAS ALREADY A DOCTOR.

THIS EARLIER TRIP--SIX WEEKS COVERING MORE THAN 4,000 KILOMETERS IN ARGENTINA-- PROVED A GOOD INTRODUCTION TO WHAT WAS TO COME.

AND HE HAD MET POVERTY ON THE ROAD.

WHERE ARE YOU HEADING?

WHEREVER THE HELL I CAN FIND WORK. AMERICAN CAN FIRED ME AFTER THREE YEARS.

HE HAD SEEN OPPRESSED ARGENTINE INDIANS LIVING IN SHANTYTOWNS.

AND HE HAD COME TO A FAR- REACHING CONCLUSION.

UNITED FRUIT COMPANY

THE WORLD'S FINEST

WE ALL SUFFER BECAUSE OF THE TERRIBLE POWER OF THE U.S. GIANT!

WE'VE GIVEN HIM SOMETHING CALLED *PENICILLIN*. I THINK IT IS HELPING.

AND ERNESTO'S ASTHMA, WHICH HAD AFFLICTED HIM SINCE HE WAS TWO YEARS OLD--AND WOULD FOR THE REST OF HIS LIFE--KEPT RETURNING.

TWO YEARS LATER, ON HIS AND ALBERTO'S MOTORCYCLE TRIP, ERNESTO'S SUFFERINGS WERE MORE PERSONAL THAN POLITICAL. A BAD CASE OF THE FLU PUT ERNESTO IN THE HOSPITAL FOR FOUR DAYS.

I...CAN...HARDLY BREATHE...MY FRIEND...

THIS DAMN CONDITION... KEPT ME OUT OF REGULAR CLASSES TILL I WAS NINE.

AND THEIR LACK OF FUNDS FORCED THEM TO GRUB FOR SLEEPING SPACE IN...

...GARAGES...

...BARNS...

SHE SMELLS WORSE THAN YOU!

...AND EVEN POLICE CELLS.

MMMM, AREN'T *YOU* HANDSOME!

ONE STORMY DAY, WHILE THEY WERE TAKING SHELTER IN A JAILHOUSE, THE WORST BLOW OF ALL CAME FROM CHICHINA.

SHE IS NOT GOING TO WAIT FOR ME.

MY DREAMS... ALL MY DREAMS HAVE COME CRASHING DOWN.

THEY HAD SPENT ALL OF FOUR WEEKS IN ARGENTINA AND WERE FINALLY CROSSING INTO CHILE.

ALBERTO, I AM READY TO CROSS INTO A NEW LIFE!

ERNESTO DID CROSS INTO A NEW LIFE...THOUGH IT HAD LESS TO DO WITH HIS LOSING CHICHINA THAN WITH WHAT HE SAW, WHICH HE RECORDED IN HIS DIARIES.

THERE IS NOT MUCH I CAN DO FOR HER.

HERE. PLEASE... TAKE OUR BLANKET.

THEY LIVE, IT SEEMS, BECAUSE IT IS A HABIT THEY CANNOT SHAKE.

NOW HE SAW, EVEN MORE VIVIDLY THAN HE HAD TWO YEARS EARLIER, THE SICK AND INCURABLE, THE WRETCHED POOR, THE HOPELESS INDIANS.

THIS YOUNG MAN, WHO WAS BORN ON JUNE 14, 1928, HAD SEEN LITTLE OF LIFE. HIS ARGENTINE ARISTOCRAT MOTHER, CELIA DE LA SERNA, AND HIS FATHER, GUEVARA LYNCH, WHO CAME FROM A ONCE WEALTHY FAMILY, HAD BROUGHT HIM UP IN A SCRUBBED-CLEAN ENVIRONMENT.

I PROMISE, ERNESTO, YOU WILL LIVE AMONG THE BEST OF OUR WORLD.

EVEN WITH THE SICKNESS THAT CONSTANTLY HAUNTED HIM...

...THAT WAS JUST ONE OF THEIR DISAGREEMENTS, WHICH SOMETIMES BECAME SHOUTING MATCHES. NOT ENOUGH MONEY, A FATHER'S PHILANDERING, A MOTHER WHO WAS A FREE-THINKING WOMAN, AND A YOUNG SON WHO COULD NOT BE DISCIPLINED.

WHY CAN'T THEY STOP? WHY CAN'T THEY LOVE EACH OTHER AS THEY ONCE DID?

HE TAKES AFTER ME. I HAD ASTHMA AS A CHILD.

OF COURSE IT'S YOU! WE ARE AT THE MERCY OF THAT DAMNED SICKNESS.

YOU'RE A FOOL, GUEVARA!

ME A FOOL? YOU WITH YOUR CIGARETTES, YOUR BOYISH PANTS, YOUR DRIVING?

8

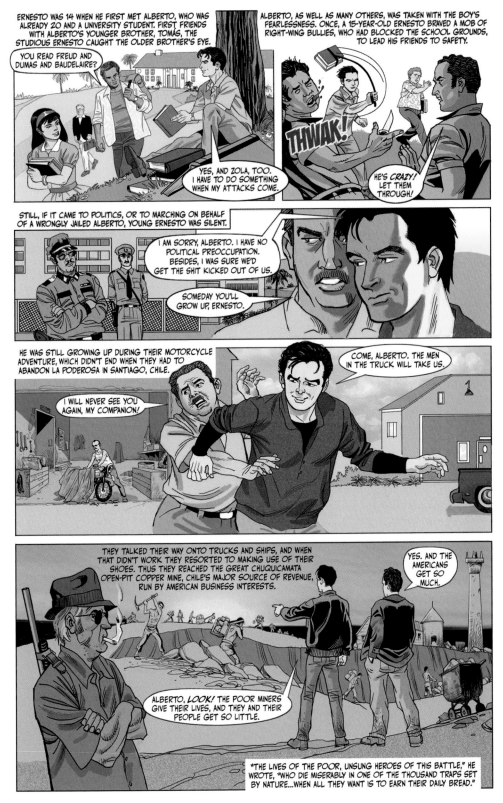

ERNESTO WAS 14 WHEN HE FIRST MET ALBERTO, WHO WAS ALREADY 20 AND A UNIVERSITY STUDENT. FIRST FRIENDS WITH ALBERTO'S YOUNGER BROTHER, TOMÁS, THE STUDIOUS ERNESTO CAUGHT THE OLDER BROTHER'S EYE.

YOU READ FREUD AND DUMAS AND BAUDELAIRE?

YES, AND ZOLA, TOO. I HAVE TO DO SOMETHING WHEN MY ATTACKS COME.

ALBERTO, AS WELL AS MANY OTHERS, WAS TAKEN WITH THE BOY'S FEARLESSNESS. ONCE, A 15-YEAR-OLD ERNESTO BRAVED A MOB OF RIGHT-WING BULLIES, WHO HAD BLOCKED THE SCHOOL GROUNDS, TO LEAD HIS FRIENDS TO SAFETY.

THWAK!

HE'S *CRAZY!* LET THEM THROUGH!

STILL, IF IT CAME TO POLITICS, OR TO MARCHING ON BEHALF OF A WRONGLY JAILED ALBERTO, YOUNG ERNESTO WAS SILENT.

I AM SORRY, ALBERTO. I HAVE NO POLITICAL PREOCCUPATION. BESIDES, I WAS SURE WE'D GET THE SHIT KICKED OUT OF US.

SOMEDAY YOU'LL GROW UP, ERNESTO.

HE WAS STILL GROWING UP DURING THEIR MOTORCYCLE ADVENTURE, WHICH DIDN'T END WHEN THEY HAD TO ABANDON LA PODEROSA IN SANTIAGO, CHILE.

I WILL NEVER SEE YOU AGAIN, MY COMPANION!

COME, ALBERTO. THE MEN IN THE TRUCK WILL TAKE US.

THEY TALKED THEIR WAY ONTO TRUCKS AND SHIPS, AND WHEN THAT DIDN'T WORK THEY RESORTED TO MAKING USE OF THEIR SHOES. THUS THEY REACHED THE GREAT CHUQUICAMATA OPEN-PIT COPPER MINE, CHILE'S MAJOR SOURCE OF REVENUE, RUN BY AMERICAN BUSINESS INTERESTS.

YES. AND THE AMERICANS GET SO MUCH.

ALBERTO, *LOOK!* THE POOR MINERS GIVE THEIR LIVES, AND THEY AND THEIR PEOPLE GET SO LITTLE.

"THE LIVES OF THE POOR, UNSUNG HEROES OF THIS BATTLE," HE WROTE, "WHO DIE MISERABLY IN ONE OF THE THOUSAND TRAPS SET BY NATURE...WHEN ALL THEY WANT IS TO EARN THEIR DAILY BREAD."

9

PERHAPS THEIR MOST IMPORTANT STOP WAS A TWO-WEEK STAY AT THE SAN PABLO LEPER COLONY ON THE AMAZON RIVER IN PERU.

ERNESTO LATER WROTE, "THE PSYCHOLOGICAL LIFT IT GIVES TO THESE POOR PEOPLE--TREATING THEM AS NORMAL HUMAN BEINGS INSTEAD OF ANIMALS, AS THEY ARE USED TO--IS INCALCULABLE."

THERE ARE 600 LEPERS WHO LIVE HERE INDEPENDENTLY AND DO WHATEVER THEY CHOOSE TO DO WHILE LOOKING AFTER THEMSELVES.

THEY JOINED THE DOCTOR ON HIS ROUNDS...

WE'RE PREPARING A STUDY OF WHAT THE DISEASE DOES TO THE NERVOUS SYSTEM.

...AND THE PATIENTS IN THEIR PLAY.

WELL DONE, ERNESTO!

WHILE THEY WERE THERE, ERNESTO CELEBRATED HIS 24TH BIRTHDAY AT A PARTY GIVEN IN HIS HONOR. AND THERE HE SAID...

THE DIVISION OF [LATIN] AMERICA INTO UNSTABLE AND ILLUSIONARY NATIONS IS COMPLETELY FICTIONAL. WE CONSTITUTE A SINGLE MESTIZO RACE. I PROPOSE A TOAST TO PERU AND TO A UNITED LATIN AMERICA!

A NEW ERNESTO GUEVARA HAD SPOKEN.

10

ERNESTO RETURNED HOME TO ARGENTINA IN AUGUST 1952. HE ALSO RETURNED TO HIS PARENTS, TO HIS STUDIES, AND TO TAKING 14 EXAMS AT THE UNIVERSITY OF BUENOS AIRES BY THE FOLLOWING MAY.

I'M SO GLAD TO HAVE YOU BACK! BUT TELL ME, HAS THE TRIP CHANGED YOU?

CHANGED HIM? WELL, AS HE LATER WROTE IN *NOTAS DE VIAJE*...

I AM NOT -- AT LEAST I CANNOT BE THE SAME AS I WAS BEFORE. THE VAGABONDING THROUGH AMERICA* HAS CHANGED ME MORE THAN I THOUGHT.

*BY AMERICA, HE MEANT HIS TRIP THROUGH SOUTH AMERICA.

ERNESTO PASSED HIS FINAL EXAM ON APRIL 11, 1953. HIS FATHER REMEMBERED THE CALL HE RECEIVED...

HELLO?

DOCTOR ERNESTO GUEVARA DE LA SERNA SPEAKING.

HOWEVER, SEVERAL DAYS BEFORE HIS 25TH BIRTHDAY, HE RECEIVED HIS DEGREE AND ANNOUNCED...

MY FRIEND CALICA AND I ARE GOING TO BOLIVIA.

REFUSING A JOB AT A LOCAL CLINIC, WHICH WOULD HAVE INCLUDED A FREE APARTMENT, ERNESTO HAD CHOSEN ANOTHER JOURNEY. SCROUNGING MONEY FROM RELATIVES, HE AND CARLOS "CALICA" FERRER TOOK THE TRAIN ON JULY 7, 1953, TO BOLIVIA AND, PERHAPS, TO PLACES UNKNOWN.

AT LEAST WE WON'T STARVE.

11

ALMOST A WEEK LATER, THEY ARRIVED IN LA PAZ, BOLIVIA, WHICH ERNESTO CALLED...

THE *SHANGHAI* OF THE AMERICAS, CALICA!

ADVENTURERS OF ALL NATIONALITIES SEEM TO FLOURISH IN THIS COLORFUL MESTIZO CITY!

SOON THEY MET FRIENDS WITH MONEY AND IMPORTANT CONTACTS, WHO IN TURN INTRODUCED THEM TO THE CITY'S CHIC AND FADDISH CABARETS.

COME HERE, TOTO!

I'D LIKE YOU TO MEET ERNESTO AND CALICA. YOU'LL *LOVE* THEM!

"THE BEST PEOPLE IN LA PAZ INVITE US TO LUNCH," CALICA WROTE TO HIS MOTHER.

"THEY DRIVE US AROUND THE CITY AND HAVE INVITED US TO A PARTY...AND THEY HAVEN'T LET US PAY FOR ANY OF THIS."

LOOK AT THEM! THESE SO-CALLED GOOD PEOPLE, THESE CULTURED ONES, WHO ARE ASTOUNDED AT EVENTS AND CURSE THE IMPORTANCE NOW GIVEN THE INDIAN AND THE CHOLO!

AT LEAST THE YOUNG BELIEVE THIS REVOLUTION IS A STEP FORWARD IN THE STRUGGLE TOWARD GREATER EQUALITY.

IT HAD FINALLY GOTTEN TO ERNESTO.

HERE IN BOLIVIA, WHICH WAS UNDERGOING REVOLUTIONARY CHANGE, HE COULD FINALLY DECIPHER THE ATTITUDES OF THE POORER CITIZENS.

HIS POLITICAL THINKING WAS BEGINNING TO TAKE SHAPE.

12

HIS THOUGHTS WERE EXPANDED DURING A TRIP HE AND CALICA TOOK TO THE BOLSA NEGRA MINE OUTSIDE LA PAZ. THIS HUGE MINE STOOD 17,000 FEET HIGH BUT WAS DWARFED BY THE NEARBY MT. ILLIMANI.

THE TWO WERE SHOWN A PLACE NEAR AN ENTRANCE WHERE, YEARS BEFORE, COMPANY GUARDS HAD MACHINE-GUNNED MINERS AND THEIR FAMILIES DURING A STRIKE.

HERE, MY FRIENDS, HERE IS WHERE THE *VERMIN* DID THEIR WORK!

NOW THAT THE STATE OWNS THE MINE, WE MINERS ARE THE STATE!

I AM MOVED, CALICA.

THE SILENCE OF THE MINE ASSAILS EVEN THOSE, LIKE US, WHO DON'T KNOW THE LANGUAGE.

THAT NIGHT, HE WROTE...

TODAY, [BOLSA NEGRA] IS THE ONLY THING THAT KEEPS BOLIVIA GOING; IT IS A MINERAL THE AMERICANS BUY, AND FOR THIS REASON THE GOVERNMENT HAS ORDERED PRODUCTION INCREASED.

THOUGH BOLIVIANS RAN THE MINE, TO ERNESTO THE AMERICANS WERE ONCE AGAIN THE MOVING FORCE.

13

LATIN AMERICA WAS IN FERMENT DURING THOSE YEARS. JUST WHAT HAD TAKEN PLACE BY THAT JULY OF 1953, AND WHAT WAS ABOUT TO HAPPEN? HERE, COUNTRY BY COUNTRY AND REGION BY REGION, IS A SNAPSHOT OF THE LATIN AMERICA THAT ERNESTO GUEVARA WAS BEGINNING TO FULLY SEE.

ECUADOR
VENEZUELA
GUYANA
COLOMBIA
SURINAME
FRENCH GUIANA
BRAZIL
PERU
BOLIVIA
PARAGUAY
CHILE
ARGENTINA
URUGUAY

ARGENTINA. CHE'S HOME COUNTRY.

COLONEL JUAN DOMINGO PERÓN, THE DRIVING FORCE BEHIND A 1943 MILITARY COUP IN ARGENTINA THAT OVERTHREW THE AUTOCRATIC REGIME OF RAMÓN CASTILLO, WOULD LATER BECOME THE NATION'S PRESIDENT. INITIALLY A SUPPORTER OF HITLER AND MUSSOLINI, HE HEADED A CONTROVERSIAL BUT OFTEN FORWARD-LOOKING REGIME.

AFTER ANOTHER OFFICER'S COUP HAD HIM JAILED IN 1945, PERÓN WAS RELEASED BY POPULAR UPRISINGS AND, WITH THE AID OF HIS WIFE, EVA, WAS OVERWHELMINGLY VICTORIOUS IN HIS ELECTION TO THE PRESIDENCY IN 1946.

CLOSED
BY ORDER OF THE GOVERNMENT

WITH EVA AS UNOFFICIAL CO-LEADER, PERÓN'S ADMINISTRATION WAS NOTED FOR MANY KINDS OF SOCIAL ADVANCES SUCH AS BETTER LABOR, EDUCATION, AND VACATION LAWS; NATIONALIZATION OF MANY INDUSTRIES; WOMEN'S SUFFRAGE (1947); AND THE WEAKENING OF AMERICAN AND BRITISH CONTROL.
BUT OVER THE YEARS, THE GOVERNMENT GREW STEADILY AUTOCRATIC...

ESPECIALLY AFTER EVA PERÓN'S DEATH FROM CANCER IN 1952 AND, AT THE SAME TIME, THE DECLINE OF THE ARGENTINE ECONOMY. THE PRESS WAS MORE AND MORE MUFFLED, AN ANTI-CLERICAL CAMPAIGN WAS STARTED BY THE GOVERNMENT, AND PERÓN'S POPULARITY FELL DRAMATICALLY.

ECUADOR
VENEZUELA
COLOMBIA
GUYANA
SURINAME
FRENCH GUIANA
PERU
BRAZIL
BOLIVIA
CHILE
PARAGUAY
ARGENTINA
URUGUAY

CHILE, ARGENTINA'S EXTREMELY THIN, 2,880-MILE-LONG WESTERN NEIGHBOR, WAS ONE OF THE NATIONS CHE VISITED AND WROTE ABOUT IN *THE MOTORCYCLE DIARIES*.

THOUGH THE NATION ENJOYED GREAT PROSPERITY UNTIL 1931, NO COUNTRY ANYWHERE SUFFERED MORE FROM THE GREAT DEPRESSION THAN CHILE, ACCORDING TO REPORTS ISSUED BY THE LEAGUE OF NATIONS. UNEMPLOYMENT IN THOSE YEARS AFFECTED ABOUT ONE-FOURTH OF THE WORKFORCE.

CLOSED UNTIL FURTHER NOTICE

CARLOS IBÁÑEZ DEL CAMPO WAS PRESIDENT FROM 1952 TO 1958. IN *THE MOTORCYCLE DIARIES*, CHE CALLED HIM "A RETIRED SOLDIER WITH DICTATORIAL TENDENCIES AND POLITICAL AMBITIONS SIMILAR TO PERÓN."

CAMPO'S AMBITIONS AND ADMINISTRATION WERE HARMED BY INFLATION AND BY CHILE'S WEAK ECONOMY.

VOTE

CHILE WAS UNIQUE IN LATIN AMERICA, AND MUCH OF THE WORLD, IN BEING ONE OF THE FEW NATIONS TO HAVE CONSISTENTLY ELECTED ITS POLITICAL LEADERS BY COMPETITIVE ELECTIONS UNINTERRUPTED BY COUPS, ASSASSINATIONS, OR REVOLUTIONS. WOMEN WERE GIVEN THE RIGHT TO VOTE IN 1949.

CHE'S MAJOR OBJECTION TO CHILE, AGAIN EXPRESSED IN *THE MOTORCYCLE DIARIES*, WAS THAT ITS COPPER MINES--THE MAIN SOURCE OF THE NATION'S INCOME--WERE RUN BY AMERICAN COMPANIES. THOUGH IBÁÑEZ, IN PREELECTION TALK, CLAIMED THAT HE WOULD NATIONALIZE THE MINES, HE NEVER DID. CHE CALLED THEIR GUIDE...

"...A FAITHFUL DOG OF THE YANKEE MASTERS."

PORTUGUESE-SPEAKING BRAZIL, THE LARGEST COUNTRY IN LATIN AMERICA, CONTAINS MORE THAN 3 MILLION SQUARE MILES, MAKING IT LARGER THAN THE UNITED STATES BY AN AREA ABOUT THE SIZE OF TEXAS.

THE BRAZILIAN CULTURE IS MARKED BY A SUCCESSFUL FUSION OF EUROPEAN, INDIAN, AND AFRICAN INFLUENCES.

A REVOLUTION IN 1930 BROUGHT GETÚLIO VARGAS TO POWER. A BENEVOLENT DICTATOR, HE HELPED BRING BRAZIL INTO THE MODERN WORLD, ENCOURAGING INDUSTRY, DIVERSIFIED AGRICULTURE, A CENTRALIZED GOVERNMENT, AND NATIONAL CONSCIOUSNESS.

VARGAS WAS FORCED OUT BY THE ARMY IN 1945, BUT THE FAILURES OF A LATER ADMINISTRATION ENABLED HIM TO RETURN TO POWER AS AN ELECTED PRESIDENT IN 1954. CHE, IN HIS MOTORCYCLE MEMOIRS, WRITES NOTHING ABOUT BRAZIL.

URUGUAY, THE SECOND SMALLEST COUNTRY IN SOUTH AMERICA, IS ON THE SOUTHERN BORDER OF BRAZIL.

ALMOST HALF OF URUGUAY'S 3.5 MILLION PEOPLE LIVE IN MONTEVIDEO, THE CAPITAL AND THE LARGEST CITY. MOST ARE OF EUROPEAN DESCENT, WITH BLACKS AND INDIANS IN THE MINORITY. BETWEEN 1903 AND 1915, UNDER THE LIBERAL ADMINISTRATION OF JOSÉ BATTLE Y ORDÓÑEZ, WOMEN WERE GIVEN THE RIGHT TO VOTE, THE DEATH PENALTY WAS ABOLISHED, AND THE LINK BETWEEN CHURCH AND STATE WAS BROKEN.

GABRIEL TERRA, WHO SEIZED POWER IN 1933 AND RULED UNTIL 1938, CONTINUED TO INCREASE SOCIAL BENEFITS. IN 1951, A NINE-MAN COUNCIL HEADED BY AN HONORARY PRESIDENT SELECTED BY THE MAJORITY PARTY RULED.

URUGUAY WAS ALSO NOT MENTIONED BY CHE.

ONE OF TWO LANDLOCKED COUNTRIES IN SOUTH AMERICA, BOLIVIA IS THE SIZE OF THE COMBINED AREAS OF TEXAS AND CALIFORNIA.

FAMOUS FOR ITS MINERAL WEALTH--PARTICULARLY TIN, BUT ALSO SILVER, COPPER, ZINC, LEAD, AND GOLD--THE STATE OF BOLIVIA WAS NAMED AFTER THE GREAT LIBERATOR SIMÓN BOLÍVAR, AND WAS ONCE A PART OF THE ANCIENT INCAN EMPIRE. MORE THAN HALF OF ITS POPULATION IS PURE INDIAN, ALTHOUGH WHITES AND *CHOLOS* (MIXED INDIAN AND WHITE) MAINTAIN ECONOMIC, POLITICAL, AND SOCIAL DOMINANCE.

SINCE BECOMING INDEPENDENT IN 1825, BOLIVIA HAS UNDERGONE MORE THAN 185 REVOLUTIONS. THE 20TH CENTURY SAW NUMEROUS MILITARY COUPS, DICTATORSHIPS, AND ECONOMIC BANKRUPTCY, WHICH LED TO FOREIGN INFLUENCE AND INTEREST IN THE COUNTRY'S MINES AND OIL FIELDS.

THOUGH DENIED VICTORY IN THE 1951 PRESIDENTIAL ELECTIONS, THE NATIONALIST REVOLUTIONARY MOVEMENT PARTY (MNR) LED A SUCCESSFUL REVOLUTION IN 1952.
THE PARTY THEN INSTITUTED A PROGRAM OF AGRARIAN REFORM, NATIONALIZED MANY OF THE TIN MINES, AND EXTENDED CIVIL RIGHTS AND SUFFRAGE TO THE INDIANS.

VOTE AQUÍ

CHE, WHO WAS CHARMED BY THE NATION'S LARGEST CITY, LA PAZ, WAS HOPEFUL FOR THE OUTCOME OF THIS REVOLUTION.

17

PERU IS ALMOST 5,000 SQUARE MILES OF DESERT, MOUNTAINS, AND LOWLANDS BORDERING ON THE PACIFIC OCEAN. ITS POPULATION IS 50 PERCENT INDIAN AND 13 PERCENT WHITE.

THE SPANISH EXPLORER FRANCISCO PIZARRO ARRIVED IN CUZCO, PERU, IN 1532 WITH A BAND OF ADVENTURERS. THEIR HORSES AND FIREARMS HELPED THEM CONQUER THE MUCH LARGER FORCES OF THE INCAN EMPIRE AND ENRICH THEMSELVES WITH SILVER AND GOLD.

RULED CONSTANTLY BY A WHITE AND MESTIZO OLIGARCHY, PERU HAD SEEN LITTLE ECONOMIC OR POLITICAL ADVANCEMENT BY THE 1950S. FOLLOWING A SUCCESSION OF PRESIDENTS AND DICTATORS, MANUEL ODRÍA, WHO LED A COUP IN 1948, REMAINED PRESIDENT UNTIL 1956.

WHILE IN LIMA, PERU'S CAPITAL, CHE SAID THAT THE CITY SYMBOLIZED "A PERU WHICH HAD NOT LEFT THE FEUDAL STATE OF THE COLONIAL ERA. IT STILL AWAITS THE BLOOD OF A TRUE EMANCIPATING REVOLUTION."

LOCATED IN THE HEART OF THE CONTINENT, LANDLOCKED PARAGUAY SUFFERED A SUCCESSION OF DICTATORSHIPS DURING THE 19TH CENTURY, AS WELL AS A DISASTROUS WAR, 1865-1870. THE 20TH CENTURY BROUGHT MANY DICTATORSHIPS, THOUGH GAINS WERE MADE IN EDUCATION, HEALTH, AND HIGHWAY CONSTRUCTION. ONE OF ITS WORST RULERS, HIGINIO MORÍNGO RULED 1940-1948.

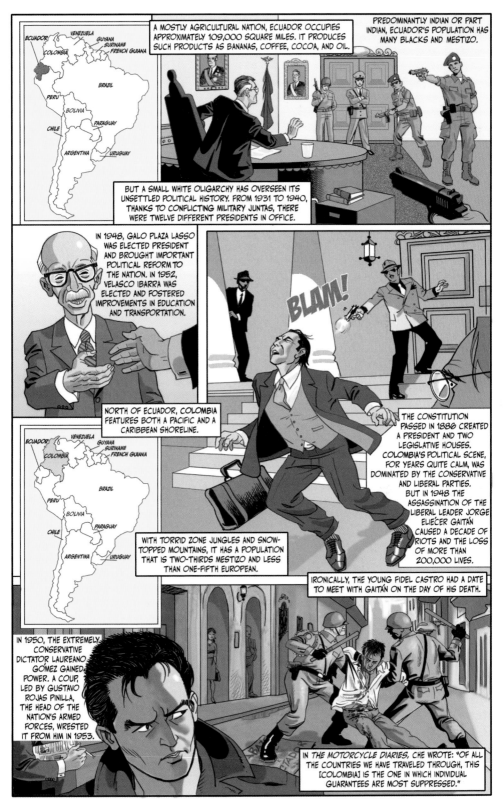

A MOSTLY AGRICULTURAL NATION, ECUADOR OCCUPIES APPROXIMATELY 109,000 SQUARE MILES. IT PRODUCES SUCH PRODUCTS AS BANANAS, COFFEE, COCOA, AND OIL.

PREDOMINANTLY INDIAN OR PART INDIAN, ECUADOR'S POPULATION HAS MANY BLACKS AND MESTIZO.

BUT A SMALL WHITE OLIGARCHY HAS OVERSEEN ITS UNSETTLED POLITICAL HISTORY. FROM 1931 TO 1940, THANKS TO CONFLICTING MILITARY JUNTAS, THERE WERE TWELVE DIFFERENT PRESIDENTS IN OFFICE.

IN 1948, GALO PLAZA LASSO WAS ELECTED PRESIDENT AND BROUGHT IMPORTANT POLITICAL REFORM TO THE NATION. IN 1952, VELASCO IBARRA WAS ELECTED AND FOSTERED IMPROVEMENTS IN EDUCATION AND TRANSPORTATION.

BLAM!

NORTH OF ECUADOR, COLOMBIA FEATURES BOTH A PACIFIC AND A CARIBBEAN SHORELINE.

THE CONSTITUTION PASSED IN 1886 CREATED A PRESIDENT AND TWO LEGISLATIVE HOUSES. COLOMBIA'S POLITICAL SCENE, FOR YEARS QUITE CALM, WAS DOMINATED BY THE CONSERVATIVE AND LIBERAL PARTIES. BUT IN 1948 THE ASSASSINATION OF THE LIBERAL LEADER JORGE ELIECER GAITÁN CAUSED A DECADE OF RIOTS AND THE LOSS OF MORE THAN 200,000 LIVES.

WITH TORRID ZONE JUNGLES AND SNOW-TOPPED MOUNTAINS, IT HAS A POPULATION THAT IS TWO-THIRDS MESTIZO AND LESS THAN ONE-FIFTH EUROPEAN.

IRONICALLY, THE YOUNG FIDEL CASTRO HAD A DATE TO MEET WITH GAITÁN ON THE DAY OF HIS DEATH.

IN 1950, THE EXTREMELY CONSERVATIVE DICTATOR LAUREANO GÓMEZ GAINED POWER. A COUP, LED BY GUSTAVO ROJAS PINILLA, THE HEAD OF THE NATION'S ARMED FORCES, WRESTED IT FROM HIM IN 1953.

IN *THE MOTORCYCLE DIARIES*, CHE WROTE: "OF ALL THE COUNTRIES WE HAVE TRAVELED THROUGH, THIS [COLOMBIA] IS THE ONE IN WHICH INDIVIDUAL GUARANTEES ARE MOST SUPPRESSED."

SITTING BETWEEN COLOMBIA AND BRAZIL, VENEZUELA ENJOYS A CARIBBEAN COASTLINE. ITS GREAT OIL BOOM HAS GIVEN IT THE HIGHEST PER CAPITA INCOME IN LATIN AMERICA, THOUGH MOST OF THE COUNTRY'S WEALTH REMAINS IN THE HANDS OF A SMALL MINORITY.

LONG IN THE CLUTCH OF DICTATORS, VENEZUELA WAS LIBERATED WHEN A MILITARY JUNTA COMMITTED TO DEMOCRACY AND, LED BY ROMULO BETANCOURT, GAINED CONTROL IN 1945. THEY CREATED A CONSTITUTION THAT PROVIDED FOR THE DIRECT POPULAR ELECTION OF THE PRESIDENT.

IN 1948, THE COUNTRY'S FIRST PRESIDENT, ROMULO GALLEGOS, WAS OVERTHROWN IN A MILITARY COUP THAT ESTABLISHED A MILITARY DICTATORSHIP.

BY 1952, COLONEL MARCOS PÉREZ JIMÉNEZ HAD BECOME DICTATOR, UTILIZING VARIOUS POLICE-STATE TECHNIQUES.

KNOWN FOR MANY YEARS AS BRITISH, DUTCH, AND FRENCH GUIANA, THE THREE FORMER POSSESSIONS ARE SIMILAR IN FORMATION, CLIMATE, FLORA, AND FAUNA.

IN APRIL 1953, CONSTITUTIONAL REFORM IN BRITISH GUIANA CREATED AN ELECTED BICAMERAL LEGISLATURE. BUT WHEN THE PEOPLE'S PROGRESSIVE PARTY (PPP) WON 18 OF THE 24 SEATS IN ONE CHAMBER, THE BRITISH GOVERNMENT SUSPENDED THE ELECTION, DEEMING THE PPP TOO FRIENDLY WITH COMMUNIST ORGANIZATIONS. IT BECAME AN INDEPENDENT NATION KNOWN AS GUYANA IN 1966.

IN 1954, DUTCH GUIANA, RENAMED SURINAME, BECAME AN AUTONOMOUS PART OF THE NETHERLANDS. IT WAS GRANTED FULL INDEPENDENCE IN MAY 1974. FAMOUS AS A FRENCH PENAL COLONY (DEVIL'S ISLAND, OFF ITS COAST, WAS WHERE ALFRED DREYFUS WAS IMPRISONED AFTER BEING FALSELY ACCUSED OF TREASON IN 1894)...

...FRENCH GUIANA BECAME AN OVERSEAS DEPARTMENT OF THE FRENCH REPUBLIC IN 1947.

CENTRAL AMERICA

CENTRAL AMERICA, WHICH INCLUDES PANAMA, COSTA RICA, NICARAGUA, HONDURAS, GUATEMALA, EL SALVADOR, AND BELIZE (FORMERLY BRITISH HONDURAS), MAKES UP THE CONNECTING ISTHMUS BETWEEN NORTH AND SOUTH AMERICA.

THE NATIONS, ONCE THE PROPERTY OF SPAIN, GAINED THEIR FREEDOM IN 1821, AND WERE BRIEFLY ANNEXED BY MEXICO. IN 1823, FIVE OF THESE ENTITIES-- GUATEMALA, EL SALVADOR, HONDURAS, NICARAGUA, AND COSTA RICA--JOINED TO FORM THE FEDERAL REPUBLIC OF CENTRAL AMERICA, MODELED AFTER THEIR NEIGHBOR, THE U.S. HOWEVER, THIS NEW ENTITY COULD NOT HOLD TOGETHER. THE UNION DISSOLVED INTO A CIVIL WAR FOUGHT BETWEEN 1833 AND 1840.

VARIOUS ATTEMPTS TO REUNIFY THE GROUP OCCURRED DURING THE 19TH CENTURY, BUT NONE SUCCEEDED FOR LONG. STILL, IN 1856-57 THE REGION SUCCESSFULLY ESTABLISHED A MILITARY COALITION TO REPEL THE INVASION LED BY THE AMERICAN ADVENTURER AND MERCENARY WILLIAM WALKER. INITIALLY FINANCED BY THE MULTIMILLIONAIRE CORNELIUS VANDERBILT, WALKER WAS INTENT ON EXPANDING AMERICA'S MANIFEST DESTINY SOUTHWARD.

DRESSED IN A LONG BLACK COAT AND A FLOPPY HAT, HE LED A MERCENARY ARMY IN AN INVASION OF NICARAGUA IN 1855. HIS FORCES JOINED A REVOLUTIONARY GROUP IN NICARAGUA AND THE COMBINED ARMIES TRIUMPHED IN 1856. PROCLAIMING HIMSELF EMPEROR, WALKER MADE ENGLISH THE OFFICIAL LANGUAGE OF NICARAGUA AND LEGALIZED SLAVERY. IN 1857, HOWEVER, HE WAS DEFEATED BY THE COMBINED FORCES OF THE OTHER CENTRAL AMERICAN NATIONS.

ON FOUR OTHER OCCASIONS, WALKER TRIED TO GAIN A FOOTHOLD IN THE AREA UNTIL FINALLY, IN 1860, THE BRITISH NAVY CAPTURED HIM AS HE TRIED TO ENTER HONDURAS. HE WAS HANDED OVER TO THE LOCAL AUTHORITIES AND EXECUTED BY A FIRING SQUAD.

MEXICO
BELIZE
HONDURAS
GUATEMALA
EL SALVADOR
NICARAGUA
COSTA RICA
PANAMA

PANAMA

THE CONNECTING LINK BETWEEN CENTRAL AND SOUTH AMERICA IS THE NATION OF PANAMA. IT OCCUPIES ABOUT 29,000 SQUARE MILES, WITH A POPULATION OF 1.5 MILLION, 70 PERCENT OF WHOM ARE MIXED RACE.

RULED BY COLOMBIA UNTIL 1903, PANAMA BECAME A SOVEREIGN NATION THROUGH U.S. INTERVENTION WHEN AMERICA DECIDED TO BUILD THE PANAMA CANAL (1904–14), CONNECTING THE ATLANTIC AND THE PACIFIC OCEANS.

THE PANAMA CANAL ZONE, A FIVE-MILE AREA ON EACH SIDE OF THE CANAL, WAS UNDER AMERICAN CONTROL AND LARGELY PEOPLED BY U.S. CITIZENS.

THE U.S. OFTEN INTERVENED IN PANAMA'S POLITICS, OSTENSIBLY TO PROTECT ITS CANAL INTERESTS. THIS CHANGED UNDER FRANKLIN DELANO ROOSEVELT'S GOOD NEIGHBOR POLICY IN THE 1930S.

BRR-RR-P!

ARNULFO ARIAS SEIZED POWER IN 1949 BUT WAS OVER-THROWN TWO YEARS LATER. JOSÉ ANTONIO REMÓN WAS ELECTED IN 1952 AND SERVED UNTIL HE WAS MACHINE-GUNNED TO DEATH AT A PANAMA CITY RACETRACK IN 1955.

COSTA RICA

LYING BETWEEN PANAMA AND NICARAGUA, THE LARGELY AGRICULTURAL NATION OF COSTA RICA CONSISTS OF CLOSE TO 20,000 SQUARE MILES AND NEARLY 2 MILLION PEOPLE, MOSTLY OF SPANISH DESCENT.

WITH A LONG DEMOCRATIC TRADITION AND A LITERACY RATE OF MORE THAN 90 PERCENT, IT IS ONE OF THE MOST STABLE OF THE LATIN AMERICAN COUNTRIES. COSTA RICA IS AN AGRICULTURAL NATION, GROWING BANANAS, COCOA, AND SUGARCANE. GAINING INDEPENDENCE FROM SPAIN IN 1821, THE SOVEREIGN REPUBLIC OF COSTA RICA WAS PROCLAIMED IN 1838. A NEW CONSTITUTION WAS ADOPTED IN 1949 AND A RULING JUNTA TRANSFERRED POWER TO OTILIO ULATE, WHO WAS PRESIDENT UNTIL 1953.

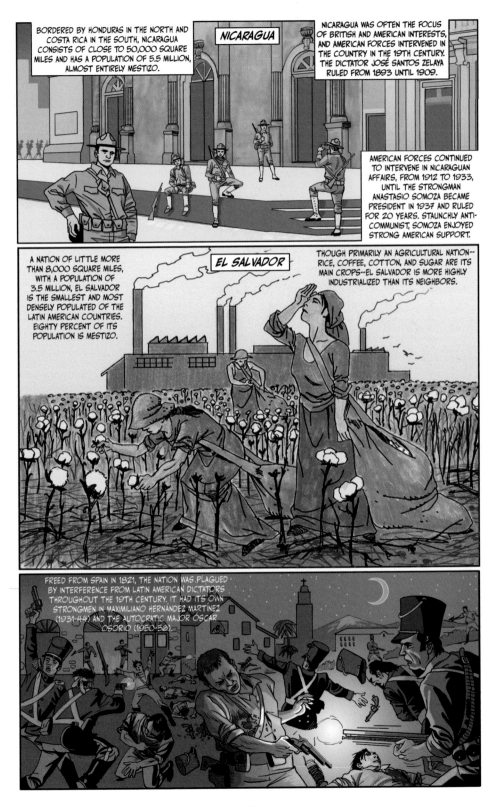

BORDERED BY HONDURAS IN THE NORTH AND COSTA RICA IN THE SOUTH, NICARAGUA CONSISTS OF CLOSE TO 50,000 SQUARE MILES AND HAS A POPULATION OF 5.5 MILLION, ALMOST ENTIRELY MESTIZO.

NICARAGUA

NICARAGUA WAS OFTEN THE FOCUS OF BRITISH AND AMERICAN INTERESTS, AND AMERICAN FORCES INTERVENED IN THE COUNTRY IN THE 19TH CENTURY. THE DICTATOR JOSÉ SANTOS ZELAYA RULED FROM 1893 UNTIL 1909.

AMERICAN FORCES CONTINUED TO INTERVENE IN NICARAGUAN AFFAIRS, FROM 1912 TO 1933, UNTIL THE STRONGMAN ANASTASIO SOMOZA BECAME PRESIDENT IN 1937 AND RULED FOR 20 YEARS. STAUNCHLY ANTI-COMMUNIST, SOMOZA ENJOYED STRONG AMERICAN SUPPORT.

A NATION OF LITTLE MORE THAN 8,000 SQUARE MILES, WITH A POPULATION OF 3.5 MILLION, EL SALVADOR IS THE SMALLEST AND MOST DENSELY POPULATED OF THE LATIN AMERICAN COUNTRIES. EIGHTY PERCENT OF ITS POPULATION IS MESTIZO.

EL SALVADOR

THOUGH PRIMARILY AN AGRICULTURAL NATION-- RICE, COFFEE, COTTON, AND SUGAR ARE ITS MAIN CROPS--EL SALVADOR IS MORE HIGHLY INDUSTRIALIZED THAN ITS NEIGHBORS.

FREED FROM SPAIN IN 1821, THE NATION WAS PLAGUED BY INTERFERENCE FROM LATIN AMERICAN DICTATORS THROUGHOUT THE 19TH CENTURY. IT HAD ITS OWN STRONGMEN IN MAXIMILIANO HERNÁNDEZ MARTÍNEZ (1931-44) AND THE AUTOCRATIC MAJOR ÓSCAR OSORIO (1950-56).

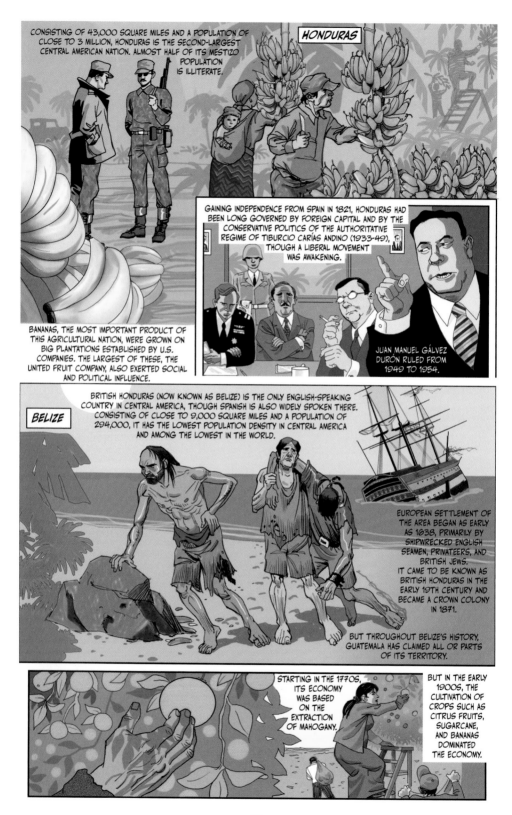

CONSISTING OF 43,000 SQUARE MILES AND A POPULATION OF CLOSE TO 3 MILLION, HONDURAS IS THE SECOND-LARGEST CENTRAL AMERICAN NATION. ALMOST HALF OF ITS MESTIZO POPULATION IS ILLITERATE.

HONDURAS

GAINING INDEPENDENCE FROM SPAIN IN 1821, HONDURAS HAD BEEN LONG GOVERNED BY FOREIGN CAPITAL AND BY THE CONSERVATIVE POLITICS OF THE AUTHORITATIVE REGIME OF TIBURCIO CARÍAS ANDINO (1933-49), THOUGH A LIBERAL MOVEMENT WAS AWAKENING.

JUAN MANUEL GÁLVEZ DURÓN RULED FROM 1949 TO 1954.

BANANAS, THE MOST IMPORTANT PRODUCT OF THIS AGRICULTURAL NATION, WERE GROWN ON BIG PLANTATIONS ESTABLISHED BY U.S. COMPANIES. THE LARGEST OF THESE, THE UNITED FRUIT COMPANY, ALSO EXERTED SOCIAL AND POLITICAL INFLUENCE.

BELIZE

BRITISH HONDURAS (NOW KNOWN AS BELIZE) IS THE ONLY ENGLISH-SPEAKING COUNTRY IN CENTRAL AMERICA, THOUGH SPANISH IS ALSO WIDELY SPOKEN THERE. CONSISTING OF CLOSE TO 9,000 SQUARE MILES AND A POPULATION OF 294,000, IT HAS THE LOWEST POPULATION DENSITY IN CENTRAL AMERICA AND AMONG THE LOWEST IN THE WORLD.

EUROPEAN SETTLEMENT OF THE AREA BEGAN AS EARLY AS 1638, PRIMARILY BY SHIPWRECKED ENGLISH SEAMEN, PRIVATEERS, AND BRITISH JEWS. IT CAME TO BE KNOWN AS BRITISH HONDURAS IN THE EARLY 19TH CENTURY AND BECAME A CROWN COLONY IN 1871.

BUT THROUGHOUT BELIZE'S HISTORY, GUATEMALA HAS CLAIMED ALL OR PARTS OF ITS TERRITORY.

STARTING IN THE 1770S, ITS ECONOMY WAS BASED ON THE EXTRACTION OF MAHOGANY.

BUT IN THE EARLY 1900S, THE CULTIVATION OF CROPS SUCH AS CITRUS FRUITS, SUGARCANE, AND BANANAS DOMINATED THE ECONOMY.

GUATEMALA

WITH AN AREA OF ALMOST 42,000 MILES--SLIGHTLY SMALLER THAN THE STATE OF TENNESSEE--AND A POPULATION OF MORE THAN 14 MILLION, GUATEMALA IS THE MOST NORTHERN OF THE CENTRAL AMERICAN NATIONS. MESTIZOS MAKE UP 60 PERCENT OF THE POPULATION, AND THE NATION HAS A LITERACY RATE OF 70 PERCENT.

AFTER BEIING PART OF THE MEXICAN EMPIRE IN THE 1820S, GUATEMALA BECAME A FULLY INDEPENDENT NATION IN THE 1840S. A "LIBERAL REVOLUTION" OCCURRED IN 1871 UNDER THE LEADERSHIP OF JUSTO RUFINO BARRIOS, WHO WITHIN 14 YEARS MODERNIZED THE NATION, INTRODUCED NEW AGRICULTURAL CROPS, AND BROUGHT IN MANUFACTURING.

THE UNITED FRUIT COMPANY BECAME A MAJOR FORCE IN GUATEMALA IN 1901 AND CONTINUED TO BE THROUGH MUCH OF THE 20TH CENTURY. UNDER THE LONG DICTATORSHIP OF GENERAL JORGE UBICO, FROM THE 1930S TO 1944, THE COMPANY BOUGHT CONTROLLING SHARES OF THE NATION'S RAILROADS, UTILITIES, AND TELEGRAPH CABLES, AS WELL AS ITS LAND.

IT'S *ALL* OURS, MY BOY! ALL *OURS!*

TEN YEARS OF POPULAR ELECTIONS AND REFORMS ENDED IN 1954, WHEN A CIA-LED REBELLION--IN THE NAME OF ANTI-COMMUNISM DURING THE HEYDAY OF THE COLD WAR--ENDED THE REGIME OF THE FREELY ELECTED JACOBO ÁRBENZ GUZMÁN. THIS OCCURRED IMMEDIATELY AFTER THE GOVERNMENT INSTITUTED DECREE NO. 900, EXPROPRIATING LARGE TRACTS OF LAND OWNED BY UNITED FRUIT.

THE REBELLION BROUGHT TO POWER COLONEL CARLOS CASTILLO ARMAS, WHO WAS INSTALLED AS PRESIDENT.

25

WITH AN AREA OF MORE THAN 750,000 SQUARE MILES AND A POPULATION OF CLOSE TO 50 MILLION, MEXICO IS THE LARGEST SPANISH-SPEAKING COUNTRY IN THE WORLD.

MEXICO

THE GREAT MAJORITY OF THE POPULACE IS OF MIXED INDIAN AND SPANISH DESCENT.

THE FIRST EUROPEANS ARRIVED IN 1517, AND THE SPANISH DEFEAT OF THE AZTECS IN 1521 BEGAN A 300-YEAR PERIOD OF SPANISH DOMINATION IN THIS REGION THEN KNOWN AS NEW SPAIN. WHEN SPAIN WAS OCCUPIED BY FRANCE IN THE EARLY 19TH CENTURY, THE CATHOLIC PRIEST MIGUEL HIDALGO Y COSTILLA DECLARED MEXICO'S INDEPENDENCE ON SEPTEMBER 16, 1810. †

RECOGNIZED BY SPAIN IN 1821, THE FIRST MEXICAN EMPIRE WAS THUS FOUNDED.

A REVOLT AGAINST EMPEROR AGUSTIN DE ITURBIDE ESTABLISHED THE UNITED MEXICAN STATES IN 1824, WITH FELIX FERNÁNDEZ AS THE FIRST PRESIDENT. MANY REBELLIONS ENSUED DURING SEVERAL ADMINISTRATIONS, LEGAL AND OTHERWISE, THROUGHOUT THE CENTURY.

THE NORTHERN STATE OF COAHUILA Y TEJAS DECLARED ITS INDEPENDENCE IN 1836, DEFEATING THE MEXICAN ARMY UNDER SANTA ANNA, AND BECOMING THE REPUBLIC OF TEXAS.

IN 1845, TEXANS VOTED TO BECOME PART OF THE U.S.

26

BORDER DISPUTES LED TO THE MEXICAN-AMERICAN WAR, 1846-48. MEXICO WAS BADLY BEATEN AS U.S. FORCES OCCUPIED MUCH OF THE NATION.

AS A RESULT, MEXICO WOULD SELL AMERICA ITS NORTHERNMOST TERRITORIES FOR THE PALTRY AMOUNT OF $15 MILLION; THESE WOULD BECOME CALIFORNIA, NEVADA, UTAH, MOST OF ARIZONA, NEW MEXICO, AND COLORADO.

IN THE 1860S, A MILITARY OCCUPATION BY FRANCE BROUGHT IN MAXIMILIAN I AS EMPEROR.
HE WAS CAPTURED AND EXECUTED BY FORCES LOYAL TO BENITO JUÁREZ, WHO REMAINED PRESIDENT UNTIL HIS DEATH IN 1872.

THE LONG REGIME OF PORFIRIO DÍAZ (1876-1911) WAS ENDED BY REVOLUTIONARY FORCES, INCLUDING SUCH LEADERS AS EMILIANO ZAPATA AND PANCHO VILLA.
SUBSEQUENTLY DURING A STRUGGLE LASTING MORE THAN 20 YEARS AND LEAVING ALMOST 900,000 PEOPLE DEAD, A VARIETY OF LEADERS LED THE NATION.

IN 1929, THE NATIONAL MEXICAN PARTY (LATER KNOWN AS THE PRI) WAS FORMED; IT RULED THE NATION FOR THE REST OF THE 20TH CENTURY.
LÁZARO CÁRDENAS, WHO BECAME PRESIDENT IN 1934, EXERTED CIVILIAN CONTROL OVER THE ARMY, SUPPORTED PROGRESSIVE POLITICS, AND NATIONALIZED THE OIL AND ELECTRICAL INDUSTRIES.

HAVANA

CUBA

THE NATION OF CUBA IS MADE UP OF CUBA, THE ISLE OF YOUTH, AND SEVERAL ADJACENT SMALL ISLANDS. IT CONTAINS MORE THAN 40,000 SQUARE MILES, AND HAD A POPULATION OF ABOUT 6.5 MILLION IN 1953. SUGARCANE HAS BEEN ITS DOMINANT CROP SINCE THE LATE 18TH CENTURY. THE ISLAND WAS DISCOVERED BY CHRISTOPHER COLUMBUS IN 1492, AND THE SPANISH CONQUEST BEGAN IN 1511.

SPAIN RULED CUBA FOR THE NEXT 388 YEARS, UNTIL THE SPANISH-AMERICAN WAR IN 1898.

AFTER FAILED ATTEMPTS BY CUBAN REVOLUTIONARIES TO GAIN INDEPENDENCE FROM SPAIN AND SIMILAR ATTEMPTS BY AMERICANS FROM THE SOUTH TO CONQUER CUBA AND MAKE IT A SLAVE STATE, IT WAS THE MYSTERIOUS SINKING OF THE USS *MAINE* IN HAVANA HARBOR ON FEBRUARY 15, 1898, THAT ULTIMATELY BROKE SPAIN'S HOLD ON THE ISLAND.

BLAMING SPAIN FOR THE SUNKEN *MAINE*-- PROBABLY ERRONEOUSLY-- THE U.S. DECLARED WAR IN JUNE AND VICTORY TWO MONTHS LATER.

AS A RESULT, CUBA BECAME AN INDEPENDENT REPUBLIC, THOUGH WITH AMERICAN OCCUPATION UNTIL 1902 AND CONSIDERABLE OVERSIGHT POWERS AFTER THAT. THIS ALLOWED U.S. INVESTORS TO CONTROL CUBA'S SUGAR TRADE AND LEFT THE U.S. IN PERMANENT CONTROL OF GUANTÁNAMO BAY.

CUBA SUFFERED FRAUDULENT ELECTIONS AND CORRUPT ADMINISTRATIONS THROUGH MUCH OF THE 20TH CENTURY. GERARDO MACHADO WAS PRESIDENT FROM 1925 TO 1933, BUT WAS OVERTHROWN WHEN HE WENT BEYOND HIS CONSTITUTIONAL TERM OF OFFICE.

THIS BROUGHT FULGENCIO BATISTA TO POWER FIRST AS PRESIDENT AND THEN AS ARMY CHIEF OF STAFF. A REVOLT LED BY FIDEL CASTRO IN 1953 WAS ABORTED BY BATISTA'S FORCES.

ERNESTO AND CALICA REMAINED IN LA PAZ FOR ABOUT A MONTH. NEVER ONCE WORKING BUT...

CHAPTER 3: BACK ON THE ROAD

IT'S ALL ON US, MY FRIENDS.

...TAKING FREE MEALS WHENEVER THEY COULD...

...ENJOYING THE COMPANY OF VARIOUS WOMEN...

I LOVE YOU, ERNESTO.

AND IF I LOVED YOU I WOULD SAY SO.

...AND MANAGING THEIR FINANCES BY SELLING THEIR BELONGINGS.

BUT MY FATHER RECENTLY BOUGHT IT FOR THREE TIMES THAT AMOUNT.

ERNESTO'S ASTHMA PERSISTED.

HIS FRIEND ANDRO HERRERO SAID, "I REMEMBER WAKING UP IN THE NIGHT WITH GUEVARA TRYING TO REACH HIS ASMAPUL [HIS MEDICINE]...

...BUT NOT HAVING THE STRENGTH TO REACH IT,

AND ONE OF US HAVING TO GET IT FOR HIM."

THOUGH ERNESTO OFTEN SPOKE ABOUT GOING TO WORK— HIS OLD FRIEND ALBERTO HAD OFFERED HIM A POSITION— AND SENDING NEEDED MONEY HOME, HE WROTE TO HIS MOTHER THAT HE HAD FOUND HIS...

...NEW POSITION AS 100 PERCENT ADVENTURER.

MEXICO

BELIZE

GUATEMALA

HONDURAS

EL SALVADOR

AND, INTRIGUED BY THE IDEA THAT THE REVOLUTION COULD SUCCEED IN GUATEMALA, HE FELL PREY TO THE PLEAS OF HIS FRIEND GUALO GARCÍA...

IT WILL CHALLENGE AMERICA'S DOMINANCE, ERNESTO. COME WITH ME TO GUATEMALA.

ERNESTO RESPONDED... "I WILL GO, GUALO!"

29

WITH CALICA GONE TO VENEZUELA TO FIND A JOB WITH THE HELP OF ALBERTO, AND ANDRO REMAINING IN ECUADOR, ERNESTO LEFT FOR GUATEMALA CITY WITH GUALO AND DOMINGO BEVERRAGI ARRIVING IN LATE DECEMBER WITH...

THREE DOLLARS BETWEEN THE THREE OF US!

SO WHAT? WE MEET THE RIGHT PEOPLE AND WE MANAGE.

THE DICTATORSHIP OF GENERAL JORGE UBICO HAD BEEN OVERTHROWN IN 1944 AND REPLACED BY A POPULAR REVOLUTIONARY GOVERNMENT HEADED FIRST BY JUAN JOSÉ ARÉVALO AND LATER BY JACOBO ÁRBENZ.

THE PROPERTIES OF THE POWERFUL UNITED FRUIT COMPANY HAD BEEN NATIONALIZED AND MANY POPULAR MEASURES HAD BEEN PASSED INTO LAW DURING THESE "TEN YEARS OF SPRING," AS THEY WERE CALLED.

UNITED FRUIT COMPANY

PROPERTY OF GUATEMALAN GOVERNMENT

ERNESTO WAS SO MOVED BY WHAT HE SAW IN GUATEMALA THAT HE QUICKLY DECIDED, "I WILL BE WITH THE PEOPLE...I PREPARED MY BEING AS IF IT WERE A SACRED PLACE SO THAT THE BESTIAL HOWLING OF THE TRIUMPHANT PROLETARIAT...CAN RESONATE WITH NEW VIBRATIONS AND NEW HOPES."

FOR THE FIRST TIME IN HIS 25 YEARS, HE FELT COMMITTED TO A CAUSE.

EARLY ON HE HAD MET HILDA GADEA, A SMALL, INTELLECTUAL, PLAIN WOMAN WHO WOULD LATER BECOME HIS WIFE.

GOOD-LOOKING, BUT TOO SUPERFICIAL TO BE INTELLIGENT.

AT FIRST, NEITHER WAS MUCH TAKEN WITH THE OTHER...

BUT HILDA WOULD INTRODUCE HIM TO MANY FIGURES WHO WERE HIGH IN GOVERNMENT.

THIS IS SEÑOR PAIZ, ERNESTO, THE MINISTER OF ECONOMY. I TOLD HIM YOU ARE SEEKING A MEDICAL POSITION.

I HAVE EXPERIENCE IN THE TREATMENT OF LEPROSY, SEÑOR.

THROUGH HILDA, HE ALSO MET SEVERAL CUBANS WHO WERE INVOLVED IN FIDEL CASTRO'S FAILED UPRISING AGAINST CUBA'S BATISTA DICTATORSHIP.

YES, FIDEL IS STILL IN THEIR RAT HOLE OF A JAIL. THEY THINK FOR 15 YEARS.

BUT HE WILL LEAD US AGAIN, AND THIS TIME WE WILL SUCCEED.

YOU PEOPLE ARE VERY BRAVE.

HILDA HAD MUCH TO OFFER ERNESTO. HER FRIENDS, HER KNOWLEDGE OF LITERATURE AND POLITICS, AND, YES, HER MONEY...

HILDA, I CAN'T TAKE ANY MORE MONEY FROM YOU.

I WILL NOT HAVE YOU SUFFER FOR LACK OF RENT MONEY.

AS SUSPICIONS GREW ABOUT U.S. INVOLVEMENT IN ATTEMPTS TO END GUATEMALA'S NEW REGIME, ERNESTO'S ANTI-U.S. FEELINGS BECAME STRONGER. IN A LETTER TO HIS FATHER, HE WROTE...

POLITICALLY, THINGS AREN'T GOING SO WELL, BECAUSE AT ANY MOMENT, A COUP IS SUSPECTED UNDER THE PATRONAGE OF YOUR FRIEND IKE.*

*PRESIDENT DWIGHT D. EISENHOWER

31

THIS GAVE THE U.S. REASON TO SUPPORT A COUP ATTEMPT AGAINST THE ÁRBENZ GOVERNMENT IN JUNE 1954.
AFTER NEARLY FAILING, THE COUP ULTIMATELY SUCCEEDED THANKS TO AMERICAN AIR SUPPORT.

STIILL WITHOUT A JOB, ERNESTO HAD FOUND A CAUSE. HE JOINED A MILITIA FORMED BY THE COMMUNIST YOUTH, AND WAS TRANSFERRED TO A HOSPITAL....

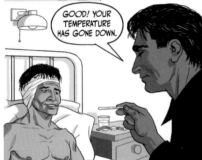

GOOD! YOUR TEMPERATURE HAS GONE DOWN.

...WHERE, DESPITE HIS DESIRE TO SERVE AT THE FRONT, HE NEVER DID.

WHEN ÁRBENZ RESIGNED HIS OFFICE ON JUNE 27, FINDING REFUGE IN THE MEXICAN EMBASSY, ERNESTO FOUND ASYLUM IN THE ARGENTINE CONSULATE.

Argentine

Consulate

KNOWN NOW AS "CHE" BECAUSE OF HIS TYPICALLY ARGENTINE HABIT OF USING THE WORD TO MEAN "HEY, YOU" OR "PAL," HE ENTERED MEXICO IN SEPTEMBER...

...SURER THAN EVER THAT THE U.S., THE "TITAN OF THE NORTH," WAS...

THE *ENEMY* OF ANY CHANGE TO THE INEQUALITY IN LATIN AMERICA!

IT IS IMPORTANT TO UNDERSTAND THE EFFECT THE COLD WAR HAD ON CHE, HIS COMPATRIOTS, AND THE LATIN AMERICAN NATIONS. THE COLD WAR WAS A CLASH OF IDEOLOGIES, PITTING AMERICA AND THE DEMOCRATIC-CAPITALIST WEST AGAINST SOVIET RUSSIA AND THE COMMUNIST EAST. THOUGH NEVER AN OVERT MILITARY CONFLICT, IT ENTAILED MASSIVE ARMS BUILDUPS (PARTICULARLY NUCLEAR WEAPONS), SEVERAL PROXY WARS, AND AGGRESSIVE INTERFERENCE IN THE OTHER'S SPHERE OF INFLUENCE.

BACKGROUND

THE YALTA CONFERENCE, HELD IN FEBRUARY 1945, MIGHT BE CONSIDERED THE INCEPTION OF THE COLD WAR. THE ALLIED LEADERS OF WORLD WAR II--U.S. PRESIDENT FRANKLIN DELANO ROOSEVELT, BRITISH PRIME MINISTER WINSTON CHURCHILL, AND SOVIET PREMIER JOSEF STALIN-- FAILED TO CREATE A MUTUALLY ACCEPTABLE FRAMEWORK FOR POSTWAR EUROPE, SETTING THE STAGE FOR THE COLD WAR.

FOLLOWING THE ALLIED VICTORY IN MAY 1945, THE SOVIET UNION OCCUPIED MUCH OF EASTERN EUROPE, WHILE THE U.S. CLAIMED MUCH OF WESTERN EUROPE. THE DEFEATED GERMANY WAS DIVIDED INTO FOUR ZONES, POLICED BY THE U.S., GREAT BRITAIN, FRANCE, AND THE SOVIET UNION.

ICELAND

SWEDEN

FINLAND

SOVIET UNION

NORWAY

ESTONIA

LATVIA

LITHUANIA

DENMARK

IRELAND

BELARUS

U.K.

NETH.

POLAND

BELGIUM

GERMANY

UKRAINE

LUXEMBOURG

CZECH SLOVAKIA

MOLDOVA

FRANCE

SWITZERLAND

AUSTRIA HUNGARY

ROMANIA

SLOVENIA

ITALY

CROATIA BOSNIA

YUGOSLAVIA

BULGARIA

MACEDONIA

SPAIN

ALBANIA

GREECE

PORTUGAL

BERLIN

WEST GERMANY

HAMBURG

EAST GERMANY

DRESDEN

BONN

FRANKFURT

MUNICH

WEST BERLIN

EAST BERLIN

IN 1949, WEST GERMANY WAS FORMED FROM THE THREE ZONES CONTROLLED BY THE WESTERN POWERS, AND THE GERMAN DEMOCRATIC REPUBLIC EMERGED FROM THE SOVIET ZONE. BERLIN, THE CAPITAL, WAS LIKEWISE SPLIT INTO PARTS.

DURING THE PRESIDENCY OF HARRY S. TRUMAN (1945-53), THE TRUMAN DOCTRINE AND THE MARSHALL PLAN WERE ADOPTED AS STRATEGIES FOR "CONTAINING" RUSSIA'S EXPANSION IN EUROPE. THE FORMER PROVIDED GREECE AND TURKEY WITH AMERICAN AID TO HELP COMBAT COMMUNIST INFLUENCE. THE LATTER OFFERED ECONOMIC ASSISTANCE TO NON-COMMUNIST EUROPEAN NATIONS, DRAWING THEM TOWARD THE WEST AND AWAY FROM THE SOVIET EAST.

THE BUCK STOPS HERE

IN JUNE 1948, THE SOVIET UNION IN EFFECT ENDED ALL GROUND AND RAIL TRAFFIC INTO WEST BERLIN. ALL ROADS WERE CLOSED "FOR REPAIRS" OR FOR "TECHNICAL DIFFICULTIES." THE WESTERN PART OF THE DIVIDED CITY WAS LEFT WITH 35 DAYS OF FOOD AND 45 DAYS OF COAL. AMERICA RESPONDED WITH AN AIRLIFT--SOON 1,500 FLIGHTS A DAY--THAT BROUGHT IN ALL NEEDED SUPPLIES.

RATHER THAN RISK WAR, THE SOVIETS CALLED OFF THE BLOCKADE ON MAY 11, 1949. THE LESSON WAS CLEAR: THE COLD WAR ALWAYS THREATENED TO TURN HOT.

IN 1949, THE U.S.-BACKED KUOMINTANG REGIME IN CHINA WAS DEFEATED BY THE RED ARMY OF MAO TSE-TUNG.
THE SOVIET UNION QUICKLY ALLIED ITSELF WITH THE PEOPLE'S REPUBLIC OF CHINA AND COMMUNISM'S GLOBAL SWAY INCREASED TREMENDOUSLY.
A PROXY WAR SOON FOLLOWED.

IN JUNE 1950, THE COMMUNIST REGIME OF NORTH KOREA ATTACKED SOUTH KOREA, ATTEMPTING TO UNITE THE NATION.

THE U.S., WITH U.N. SUPPORT, ENTERED THE WAR IN 1950 ON THE SIDE OF THE SOUTH. LATER THAT YEAR, CHINA ENTERED ON THE SIDE OF THE NORTH.
THE WAR ENDED IN A STALEMATE IN 1953.

IN JANUARY 1953, DWIGHT D. EISENHOWER WAS INAUGURATED AS THE NEXT AMERICAN PRESIDENT.

IN THE SOVIET UNION, JOSEF STALIN DIED IN MARCH OF THAT YEAR, AND NIKITA KHRUSHCHEV BECAME PREMIER. BUT THE COLD WAR DID NOT SUBSIDE.

ALARMED BY EUROPE'S EAST-WEST DIVIDE, THE "LOSS" OF CHINA, THE BLOODSHED IN KOREA, AND THE SOVIET ADVANCES IN WEAPONS AND TECHNOLOGY, AMERICA WAS DETERMINED THAT ANY THREAT OF COMMUNISM IN ITS HEMISPHERE WOULD BE MET WITH RESISTANCE--OPENLY OR COVERTLY.

37

40

LABELED "THE ARGENTINE DOCTOR ERNESTO GUEVARA DE LA SERNA," CHE WAS JAILED FOR THE LONGEST TIME AND WAS CONSIDERED THE MOST IMPORTANT SUSPECT. "THE PRINCIPAL LINK," IT WAS SUPPOSED, "BETWEEN THE CUBAN PLOTTERS AND CERTAIN COMMUNIST ORGANIZATIONS OF AN INTERNATIONAL NATURE."

ERNESTO GUEVARA DE LA SERNA
DOCTOR REVOLUTIONARY
ARGENTINE

HE WROTE TO HIS PARENTS FROM JAIL TWO WEEKS LATER, SAYING...

"MY FUTURE IS LINKED WITH THAT OF THE CUBAN REVOLUTION. I EITHER TRIUMPH WITH IT OR DIE THERE..."

ALTHOUGH THEY WERE ALL JAILED FOR IMMIGRATION VIOLATIONS, THE MEXICAN PRESS WAS FILLED WITH STORIES ABOUT THEIR SUPPOSED PARTICIPATION IN A CUBAN PLOT. LABELING THE ACCUSATIONS "ABSURD," FIDEL WAS RELEASED ON JULY 24.

POSSIBLY WITH THE HELP OF A BRIBE FROM FIDEL, CHE AND CALIXTO GARCÍA, THE LAST OF THOSE IMPRISONED, WERE RELEASED IN MID-AUGUST.

AND MY NAME IS ERNESTO GONZALES.

RELEASED FROM PRISON ON CONDITION THAT THEY LEAVE MEXICO WITHIN DAYS, CALIXTO AND CHE, ON FIDEL'S ORDERS, WENT INTO HIDING USING FALSE NAMES AT A WEEKEND RETREAT.

Mundo

HILDA AND THE BABY WOULD OFTEN VISIT CHE, AND ONCE SHE FOUND HIM TELLING THE CHILD...

MY LITTLE *MAO*, YOU DON'T KNOW WHAT A DIFFICULT WORLD YOU'RE GOING TO HAVE TO LIVE IN.

MAYBE THE WHOLE WORLD WILL BE FIGHTING AGAINST THE GREAT ENEMY-- YANKEE IMPERIALISM!

MEANWHILE, IN SEPTEMBER, FIDEL TRAVELED TO TEXAS TO MEET THE DEPOSED CUBAN PRESIDENT CARLOS PRÍO SOCARRÁS, A FORMER POLITICAL FOE.

I WILL SUPPORT YOUR INVASION WITH CASH, FIDEL. FIFTY THOUSAND NOW, MORE LATER.

MANY HAVE SUGGESTED THIS WAS CIA MONEY, BUT IT HAS NEVER BEEN PROVEN.

FIDEL SOON PUT THIS MONEY TO WORK WITH THE AMERICAN ÉMIGRÉ ROBERT ERICKSON.

THE RUN-DOWN 38-FOOT MOTOR YACHT, CALLED THE *GRANMA*, NEEDED WORK AND WAS SMALLER THAN FIDEL HAD HOPED FOR. BUT FOR $40,000 HE BOUGHT THE SHIP AS WELL AS A NEARBY HOUSE.

LET ME SEE THE BOAT, MR. ERICKSON. IF IT CAN BE MADE SEAWORTHY, YOU'VE GOT A DEAL.

GRANMA

AND HE PUT HIS MEN TO WORK FIXING THE SHIP.

IT TOOK UNTIL NOVEMBER FOR WORK ON THE *GRANMA* TO BE FINISHED.

IT IS DONE. WE ARE READY FOR THE NEXT STEP!

FINALLY, ON NOVEMBER 23, FIDEL CASTRO DECIDED...

THE DAY HAS COME! WE GO TO WORK!

THE WORD WENT OUT TO REBELS SHELTERED IN MEXICAN CITIES--VERACRUZ, MEXICO CITY, TAMAULIPAS--TO MEET IMMEDIATELY IN THE TOWN OF TUXPAN.

HURRY, CHE, WE ARE WAITING FOR YOU!

AND IN THE MORNING OF NOVEMBER 25, 1956, THE *GRANMA*, NOW CARRYING AN OVERLOADED CARGO OF 82 MEN, GUNS, AND ALL SORTS OF EQUIPMENT, PLODDED DOWN THE RIVER TOWARD THE GULF OF MEXICO AND THEIR DESTINATION: *CUBA!*

43

THE ADVENTURE WAS A CATACLYSMIC FAILURE. CALCULATED TO TAKE FIVE DAYS, THE JOURNEY TO CUBA TOOK SEVEN.

IN ADDITION, THE PLAN TO MEET UP WITH A REBEL GROUP IN SANTIAGO FAILED BECAUSE THE *GRANMA* WAS FORCED TO LAND A MILE AWAY FROM ITS DESIGNATED SITE, NEAR MANZANILLO.

CHAPTER 4: CUBA

HAVANA

CUBA

MANZANILLO

SIERRA MAESTRA

SANTIAGO

THE REBELS IN SANTIAGO WERE CRUSHED, AND FIDEL'S FORCES, SPOTTED WHILE CROSSING FROM MEXICO, WERE HIT HARD BY GOVERNMENT TROOPS AS THEY REACHED LAND.

OF THE 82 MEN WHO STARTED THE INVASION, ONLY 22 SURVIVED, AND THEY HAD VERY FEW ARMS AND SUPPLIES.

CHE, WHO HAD BEEN WOUNDED SUPERFICIALLY IN THE NECK, WAS ONE OF THE SURVIVORS. PART OF A GROUP OF EIGHT MEN, HE TRAVELED AT NIGHT MOVING EASTWARD.

A GUIDE FOUND THE MEN, INFORMED THEM THAT FIDEL AND RAÚL WERE SAFE, AND LED THEM TO FIDEL'S CAMP IN LATE DECEMBER. FIDEL HAD BEEN MAKING PLANS FOR CONTINUING THEIR STRUGGLE.

45

"[Fidel Castro] is alive and fighting hard and successfully in the rugged, almost impenetrable vastness of the Sierra Maestra...

From the look of things, General Batista cannot possibly hope to suppress the Castro revolt...This was quite a man-- a powerful six-footer, olive-skinned, full-faced, with a scraggly beard...It is a revolutionary movement that calls itself socialistic...It amounts to a new deal for Cuba, radical, democratic and therefore anti-communist."

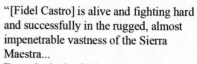

BY THE MIDDLE OF MARCH 1957, 50 RECRUITS WITH WEAPONS HAD ARRIVED, AND THE ORIGINAL GROUP OF 18 MEN WAS NOW MORE THAN DOUBLE IN SIZE.

A SECOND INTERVIEW OF FIDEL BY ROBERT TABER OF CBS TOOK PLACE ON APRIL 28. IT WAS HELD AT THE TOP OF MT. TURQUINO, THE NATION'S TALLEST PEAK, AND BROUGHT FURTHER ACCLAIM AND MORE RECRUITS FOR THE REBELS.

NOW WITH 127 WELL-ARMED MEN, FIDEL'S FORCES ATTACKED A CUBAN ARMY GARRISON AT EL UVERO, KILLING 14, WOUNDING 19, AND TAKING 14 PRISONERS.

THE GARRISON SURRENDERED, AND, ACCORDING TO CHE, THE BATTLE WAS A TURNING POINT IN THE REBELLION. "FOR US," HE SAID, "THIS WAS THE VICTORY THAT MARKED OUR COMING OF AGE."

DURING THIS BATTLE AND SEVERAL THAT FOLLOWED, CHE WAS A VALIANT SOLDIER ONE MOMENT AND A DOCTOR TREATING THE WOUNDED THE NEXT.

I BARELY HAVE TIME TO WASH MY HANDS!

HE LED HIS CONTINGENT OF MEN SAFELY INTO THE MOUNTAINS TOWARD MT. TURQUINO AND A JUNE 17 MEETING WITH FIDEL, WHO BY THAT TIME HAD AN ARMY OF 200 MEN.

FOR HIS COURAGE AND ACCOMPLISHMENTS, CHE WAS PROMOTED TO CAPTAIN AND GIVEN HIS FIRST MILITARY COMMAND--MORE THAN 75 MEN THIS TIME.

LITTLE MORE THAN A MONTH LATER, HE RECEIVED A SECOND PROMOTION. HE WAS NAMED COMMANDANT OF THE NOW ACTUAL SECOND COLUMN OF THE GUERRILLA ARMY, THE GROUP'S HIGHEST RANK. EQUIVALENT TO THE RANK OF MAJOR, THIS POSITION WAS HELD ONLY BY CHE AND FIDEL CASTRO.

IN THE REMAINING MONTHS OF 1957, ONLY MINOR SKIRMISHES WERE FOUGHT WITH THE BATISTA ARMY. HOLDING ON TO THEIR POSITIONS IN THE MOUNTAINS, THE REBELS MADE NO SIGNIFICANT ADVANCES.

RAK-AT-AK-AK-

BLAM! BAM!

INSTEAD, A MAJOR BATTLE TOOK PLACE ON THE POLITICAL FRONT. ON NOVEMBER 1, VARIOUS ANTI-BATISTA GROUPS FORMED A "CUBAN LIBERATION JUNTA" IN MIAMI. IT EXCLUDED COMMUNISTS AND, IN FIDEL'S EYES, LESSENED HIS IMPORTANCE.

AFTER OUR VICTORY, THE REBELS CAN BE MADE PART OF CUBA'S ARMED FORCES.

GOOD! AND WE MUST MAKE SURE NOT TO INSULT THE AMERICANS.

WITH CHE'S TOTAL AGREEMENT, FIDEL ANSWERED THE MEMBERS OF THE PACT, SAYING THAT THE STRUGGLE'S LEADERSHIP WOULD REMAIN...

...IN THE HANDS OF THE REVOLUTIONARY FIGHTERS. THE JULY 26 MOVEMENT CLAIMS FOR ITSELF THE ROLE OF MAINTAINING PUBLIC ORDER AND REORGANIZING THE ARMED FORCES.

IN THE EARLY MONTHS OF 1958, NEWSPAPER CORRESPONDENTS FROM THE U.S., LATIN AMERICA, AND EVEN *PARIS MATCH* INTERVIEWED THE REBEL LEADER.

DO YOU REALIZE YOUR MOVEMENT IS SPOKEN ABOUT ALL OVER THE WORLD?

WHAT ARE YOU STRIVING FOR?

FIDEL'S ANSWERS WERE SCOURED CLEAN. HE WAS FOR FREE ENTERPRISE AND FREE ELECTIONS, AND HE CERTAINLY WAS NOT A COMMUNIST.

IN MID-FEBRUARY OF 1958, IN AN IMPORTANT STRIKE, THE REBELS ATTACKED PINO DEL AGUA, AN AREA HOUSING AN ENTIRE CUBAN ARMY COMPANY THAT FIDEL HOPED TO DESTROY.
AFTER AN INITIAL SETBACK, THE REBELS CAUSED SUBSTANTIAL DAMAGE AND LOSS OF LIFE.

BUT THE BATTLE QUICKLY TURNED AROUND, AS FIDEL'S FORCES RETREATED IN THE FACE OF STRAFING GOVERNMENT PLANES.

48

AT THE END OF FEBRUARY, FIDEL AGAIN MISREPRESENTED HIS FORCES. BY NAMING HIS BROTHER RAÚL AND TWO OTHER LIEUTENANTS COMMANDANTS, HE EXAGGERATED THE SIZE OF THE FORCES THEY LED.

I WILL TELL THEM THAT YOU, RAÚL, WILL OPEN A SECOND EASTERN FRONT, AND YOU, JUAN...

SOON AFTER THAT, HE GAVE CHE A NEW AND CRITICAL ROLE.

I WANT A TRAINING SCHOOL CREATED HERE AT MINAS DEL FRIO THAT YOU WILL DEVELOP FOR BOTH VOLUNTEERS AND OFFICERS.

YOU CAN USE EVELIO LAFFERTE TO RUN ITS DAILY OPERATIONS.

THE URUGUAYAN JOURNALIST CARLOS MARÍA GUTIÉRREZ, WHO VISITED THE REBEL CAMP IN SIERRA MAESTRA, WAS IMPRESSED WITH THE RAPPORT BETWEEN CHE AND THE MEN.

"THERE WERE NO ORDERS, NOR PERMISSIONS, NOR MILITARY PROTOCOL."

"FIDEL, CHE, AND THE OTHERS LIVED IN THE SAME PLACE."

"[IN] COMBAT [THEY] FIRED FROM THE SAME LINE."

WHEN ARGENTINE NEWSMAN JORGE RICARDO MASETTI ASKED WHY THIS ARGENTINE MAN WAS FIGHTING IN ANOTHER LAND, CHE ANSWERED...

I CONSIDER MY FATHERLAND TO BE NOT ONLY ARGENTINA BUT ALL OF AMERICA.

NO COUNTRY UNTIL NOW HAS DENOUNCED AMERICA'S INTERFERENCE IN CUBAN AFFAIRS, NOR HAS A SINGLE DAILY NEWSPAPER ACCUSED THE YANKEES OF HELPING BATISTA MASSACRE HIS OWN PEOPLE.

THOSE WHO PROVIDE THE ARMS FOR CIVIL WAR AREN'T MEDDLERS. I AM.

49

NOW AWARE OF HIS SON'S GROWING CELEBRITY, CHE'S PROUD FATHER TRANSFORMED HIS HOUSE INTO A "REVOLUTIONARY CENTER."

YES, CHE IS MY SON. AND I AM WITH HIM!

Centro Revolucionario

CHE'S WIFE, HILDA, REPRESENTED THE JULY 26 MOVEMENT IN PERU, WHILE CHAPTERS SPREAD ALL OVER THE U.S. AND LATIN AMERICA.

BUT IN EARLY APRIL AN ATTEMPT BY FIDEL TO LAUNCH A GENERAL STRIKE IN CUBA AND PARALYZE THE NATION FAILED COMPLETELY.

HADN'T CASTRO ASKED FOR A GENERAL STRIKE TODAY?

CASTRO? WHO IS THIS CASTRO?

IT WAS A GRAVE SETBACK FOR THE REBELS.

A POSSIBLE REVOLT WITHIN THE MOVEMENT BECAUSE OF THIS FAILURE WAS DEFEATED BY SEVERAL OF CHE'S PROPOSALS AT A DECISIVE MEETING.

YES, ERRORS MAY HAVE BEEN COMMITED.

BUT HERE WITH US AT THE SIERRAS CAN BE THE ONLY AUTHORITATIVE LEADERSHIP, AND FIDEL CASTRO THE ONE COMMANDER IN CHIEF!

CHE'S PROPOSALS WERE AGREED TO JUST IN TIME FOR THE BATISTA GOVERNMENT'S HUGE OFFENSIVE IN MAY.

TROOPS LANDED AT TWO PLACES ALONG THE COAST.

TROOPS OVERRAN INLAND FARMS.

PLANES AND SHIPS BOMBARDED LA PLATA.

AND FIDEL CASTRO WONDERED IF HIS FORCES COULD WITHSTAND THE ONSLAUGHT.

TOWARD THE END OF MAY, THE BATISTA FORCES, UNDER GENERAL
EULOGIO CANTILLO--ABOUT 10,000 STRONG--HAD ENCIRCLED
THE REBEL AREA BY LAND AND BY SEA.
AT THAT POINT, THE REBEL ARMY CONTAINED ABOUT 280 FIGHTERS
DEFENDING AN AREA OF ONLY SEVERAL SQUARE MILES.

UNDER SIEGE DURING THE FOLLOWING
THREE MONTHS, CHE ENLISTED
VOLUNTEERS FROM WHEREVER HE
COULD TO FIGHT AND TO BUILD
FORTIFICATIONS, INCREASING THE
NUMBERS OF HIS ORIGINAL GROUP.

LAS VEGAS
DE JIBACOA

LA PLATA

MOMBEI

MINAS DEL
FRIO

GOVERNMENT FORCES ADVANCED ON MOST
FRONTS, TIGHTENING THE NOOSE. TOWARD
THE END OF JUNE, HOWEVER, THE REBELS
STOPPED THE TROOPS AT ONE POINT,
SEIZING 22 SOLDIERS AND MANY WEAPONS.

AND
WHERE
DO
YOU
GO
NOW?

BUT THE TERRAIN CHECKED THE GOVERNMENT
FORCES MORE THAN THE REBEL FIGHTERS DID.
MASSIVE WOODLANDS AND WIDE CHASMS OFTEN
BLOCKED THEIR PATH, FORCING THEM TO RETREAT,
SOMETIMES INTO THE ARMS OF THE REBELS.

ANOTHER OF FIDEL'S TRICKS HELPED LEAD TO HIS GREATEST VICTORY SO FAR IN THE WAR. ONE OF HIS MEN, PRETENDING TO BE A BATISTA RADIO OFFICER, INFORMED THE AIR FORCE...

WE MUST *STOP* THEM! THE REBELS HAVE TAKEN THE CAMP AT JIGÜE!

WHICH, OF COURSE, THE REBELS HADN'T.

A FEW DAYS AFTERWARD, FIDEL'S FORCES CAPTURED 42 MEN AND A HAUL OF WEAPONS.

AND TWO DAYS LATER THE GOVERNMENT'S COMMANDING OFFICER SURRENDERED WITH HIS REMAINING FORCE, A LANDMARK VICTORY.

BUT THE AIR FORCE RESPONDED, KILLING AND WOUNDING THEIR OWN MEN.

IT WAS ANOTHER VICTORY, AS FIDEL'S FORCES TURNED BACK AND DEFEATED AN OVERWHELMINGLY LARGER FORCE.

ON JULY 20, THE CARACAS PACT WAS DISCLOSED, BRINGING FIDEL ANOTHER VICTORY. THE AGREEMENT UNIFIED EIGHT DIFFERENT GROUPS OPPOSED TO BATISTA AND NAMED CASTRO "COMMANDER IN CHIEF OF REVOLUTIONARY FORCES."

THE PACT EXCLUDED THE *PSP* (THE PARTIDO SOCIALISTA), CUBA'S COMMUNIST PARTY. THE *PSP* WAS CONSIDERED A THREAT TO REBEL UNITY AND A PUBLIC RELATIONS RISK.

CHE LATER WROTE OF THE WAR AT THAT TIME...

BATISTA'S ARMY CAME OUT OF THAT LAST OFFENSIVE IN SIERRA MAESTRA WITH ITS SPINE BROKEN, BUT IT HAD NOT YET BEEN DEFEATED. THE STRUGGLE WOULD GO ON.

CUBA'S RELENTLESS RAINY SEASON AFFLICTED CHE'S REBEL FORCES DURING THE NEXT MONTH AND A HALF, WHILE BATISTA'S ARMY TRAILED THEM AND HIS AIR FORCE ATTACKED. ACCORDING TO CHE, THEY FACED...

...HUNGER, THIRST, WEARINESS, A FEELING OF IMPOTENCE AGAINST THE ENEMY FORCES THAT WERE INCREASINGLY CLOSING IN ON US.

STILL, CHE'S FORCES CROSSED ALMOST 400 MILES TO REACH THE FARMLANDS OF ESCAMBRAY.

THOUGH AWARE THAT THE GOVERNMENT WAS SEEKING WAYS TO MAKE PUBLIC HIS COMMUNIST PARTY TIES, CHE MET WITH COMMUNIST PARTY OFFICIALS IN ESCAMBRAY.

"I WAS STRUCK BY HIS PERSONALITY AND BY THE RESPECT EVERYONE GAVE HIM," SAID PARTY OFFICIAL OVIDIO DÍAZ RODRÍGUEZ, WHOSE OWN ADMIRATION FOR CHE ONLY "INCREASED."

FIDEL HAD ORDERED CHE TO UNIFY THE FEUDING REBEL GROUPS OF THE AREA: THE SECOND FRONT, THE DIRECTORIO, AND SEVERAL FACTIONS OF THEIR OWN JULY 26 MOVEMENT.

WE MUST TRY TO BRING THESE BICKERING *FOOLS* TOGETHER!

ALTHOUGH CHE WAS NOT A COMPLETE SUCCESS, HE ACCOMPLISHED MUCH--THE DIRECTORIO, FOR ONE, ACCEPTED UNITY WITH CHE--AND CERTAINLY THINGS HAD BEEN SMOOTHED INSIDE THE JULY 26 MOVEMENT.

IN REFERENCE TO A MEETING WITH CHE, LOCAL LEADER ENRIQUE OLTULSKI LATER WROTE...

"CHE SMOKED AND COUGHED A DAMP COUGH...HE SMELLED BAD. HE SMELLED OF DECOMPOSED SWEAT...[BUT] IN SPITE OF EVERYTHING, ONE CAN'T HELP ADMIRING HIM. HE KNOWS WHAT HE WANTS BETTER THAN WE DO. AND HE LIVES ENTIRELY FOR IT."

JOSÉ MARTÍ

IN NOVEMBER, ALEIDA MARCH ENTERED CHE'S LIFE. ON A MISSION FOR THE LAS VILLAS REBELS, SHE WAS THE BEAUTIFUL 24-YEAR-OLD DAUGHTER OF A POOR BUT EDUCATED FAMILY WHO WAS HERSELF A COLLEGE GRADUATE.

SHE AND CHE SOON FELL IN LOVE, AND FROM THE START OF THEIR AFFAIR, ALEIDA CLAIMED, "I NEVER LEFT HIS SIDE."

LATER THAT MONTH, A COMBINED ATTACK BY THE CUBAN AIR FORCE AND THE ARMY AT THREE DIFFERENT POINTS TURNED INTO A BATTLE THAT LASTED FOR SIX DAYS.

WHEN IT WAS OVER, THE CUBAN ARMY WAS THROWN BACK, MUCH OF ITS ARMAMENT HAD BEEN CAPTURED, AND TWO IMPORTANT BRIDGES HAD BEEN DESTROYED.

AS DECEMBER CAME TO A CLOSE, CHE'S FORCES AND THOSE OF SEVERAL OF HIS ALLIES TOOK TOWN AFTER TOWN IN THE PROVINCE, AND PREPARED FOR THE INVASION OF SANTA CLARA, THE NATION'S FOURTH LARGEST CITY.

AND NOW, SANTA CLARA!

AT THAT TIME, FIDEL WROTE TO HIS TOP COMMANDER, "THE WAR IS WON. THE ENEMY IS COLLAPSING WITH A RESOUNDING CRASH...ALL THIS IS THE RESULT OF ONE THING: OUR DETERMINED EFFORT...IT IS SUPREMELY IMPORTANT THAT THE ADVANCE TOWARD MATANZAS AND HAVANA BE CARRIED OUT EXCLUSIVELY BY THE 26TH OF JULY FORCES."

AND WHILE REBEL FORCES OCCUPIED CITY AFTER CITY, WITH CROWDS HAPPILY WELCOMING THEM, BATISTA READIED PLANES TO EVACUATE HIMSELF AND HIS SUPPORTERS TO SAFETY.

THE END CAME SWIFTLY. AT THE CLOSE OF DECEMBER, REBEL FORCES UNDER CHE'S COMMAND MOVED DEEP INTO SANTA CLARA, THE SITE OF BATISTA'S LAST DEFENSE.

THEY CAPTURED THE CITY'S TRAIN STATION, AND AS A TRAIN OF 22 CARS LOADED WITH SOLDIERS AND AMMUNITION ATTEMPTED TO ESCAPE...

...IT WAS DERAILED, THE TRACKS HAVING BEEN BLOWN UP BY HOMEMADE BOMBS SET BY THE REBELLING CITIZENRY; IT CRUMBLED INTO A MESS OF METAL AND DEATH.

THE GOVERNMENT HAD BEEN DEFEATED, THE REVOLUTION WON.

ON JANUARY 2, 1959, CHE AND CAMILO CIENFUEGOS LED THEIR SEPARATE FORCES TOWARD HAVANA AND TO FINAL VICTORY.

CHAPTER 5: VICTORY

IN ONE OF CASTRO'S FIRST MOVES, HE NAMED MANUEL URRUTIA --A LIBERAL LAWYER AND LEADER IN THE RESISTANCE MOVEMENT-- PRESIDENT. THIS SEEMED AN ATTEMPT TO GAIN U.S. SUPPORT FOR THE NEW GOVERNMENT.

THOUGH URRUTIA WAS PRESIDENT, HE WAS ALLOWED TO APPOINT ONLY THE JUSTICE MINISTER. CASTRO, NOW COMMANDER IN CHIEF, MADE ALL OTHER APPOINTMENTS.

IN EARLY JANUARY, CASTRO RODE TRIUMPHANTLY THROUGH THE STREETS OF HAVANA ATOP A CAPTURED ENEMY TANK...

AS CROWDS WENT WILD.

VIVA FIDEL!

HE AND URRUTIA IMMEDIATELY WENT TO WORK REFORMING THE CONSTITUTION, REORGANIZING THE ARMY, AND CLEANING UP CRIME IN SEX-DRIVEN HAVANA.

DURING THOSE EARLY DAYS OF VICTORY, CASTRO APPARENTLY FELT THAT IT WAS IMPORTANT TO KEEP HIS TWO WELL-KNOWN RADICALS--CHE AND HIS BROTHER RAÚL--OUT OF THE LIMELIGHT.

A GREAT NATIONAL HERO BECAUSE OF HIS WARTIME EXPLOITS, CHE WAS MADE SUPREME PROSECUTOR OF THE MORE THAN A THOUSAND WAR CRIMINALS WHO HAD BEEN CAPTURED.

A LARGE NUMBER WERE EXECUTED BY HIS ORDERS, SPARKING PROTEST FROM MANY FOREIGN OFFICIALS.

ONE REPORT CLAIMED THAT THERE WERE 156 EXECUTIONS, ANOTHER PLACED THE FIGURE AT "ABOUT 550."

SO CHE WAS NAMED COMMANDER OF LA CABAÑA, THE HUGE FORTRESS OVERLOOKING HAVANA.

AND RAÚL WAS MADE MILITARY GOVERNOR OF ORIENTE.

DESPITE ACCUSATIONS TO THE CONTRARY, JON LEE ANDERSON, THE AUTHOR OF *CHE GUEVARA: A REVOLUTIONARY LIFE,* ONE OF THE LEADING CHE BIOGRAPHIES, HAS SAID, "I HAVE YET TO FIND A SINGLE CREDIBLE SOURCE POINTING TO A CASE WHERE CHE EXECUTED AN INNOCENT."

ON FEBRUARY 16, 1959, CASTRO WAS SWORN IN AS PRIME MINISTER AND, IN TRUTH, BECAME THE LEADER OF THE NEW CUBAN GOVERNMENT.
ONE DAY LATER, CHE GUEVARA WAS ALSO ACCORDED A GREAT HONOR WHEN HE WAS PROCLAIMED "A CITIZEN OF BIRTH" OF CUBA.

AND IN MID-APRIL, ACCOMPANIED BY A GROUP OF CONSERVATIVES AND PRO-AMERICAN AIDES (CHE AND RAÚL WERE LEFT BEHIND), CASTRO WENT TO THE U.S. ON A GOODWILL TOUR.

ALTHOUGH HE DENIED ALL COMMUNIST TIES, OR THAT HE HAD PROVIDED AID TO OTHER LATIN AMERICAN REBELS, CASTRO WAS DESCRIBED BY VICE PRESIDENT RICHARD NIXON AS...

...INCREDIBLY NAIVE.

TRAVELING IN THE U.S., CASTRO MAINTAINED THAT CUBA WAS NOT A COMMUNIST COUNTRY. WHEN TWO CUBANS WERE CAUGHT IN A REVOLUTIONARY PLOT AGAINST PANAMA, HE CALLED THEM "IRRESPONSIBLE" AND SAID THAT CUBA...

...DID NOT EXPORT REVOLUTION.

IT WAS CHE, HOWEVER, WHO OCCASIONED THE MOST SCATHING COMMENTS. WHITING WILLAUER, THE U.S. AMBASSADOR TO COSTA RICA, SAID IN A LETTER TO A STATE DEPARTMENT OFFICIAL, "CASTRO'S DENIALS OF COMMUNIST LINKS" COULD BE BELIEVED "WHEN AND ONLY WHEN CHE GUEVARA AND THE OTHER TOP COMMUNISTS ARE GIVEN A ONE-WAY TICKET OUT OF THE COUNTRY."

AT LEAST CHE'S LIFE WAS MADE HAPPIER AND SIMPLER. ON MAY 22, 1959, HE WAS GRANTED AN AMICABLE DIVORCE FROM HILDA, AND ON JUNE 2 CHE AND ALEIDA MARCH WERE MARRIED IN A CIVIL CEREMONY.

I WILL DO THE BEST I CAN TO INCREASE OUR TRADE.

I DO.

AND TEN DAYS LATER, STANDING AGAIN AS COMMANDANT OF THE REVOLUTIONARY FORCES, CHE BEGAN A THREE-MONTH TOUR OF NON-ALIGNED NATIONS AT CASTRO'S BEHEST.

BACKGROUND: THE NON-ALIGNED NATIONS

JOSIP BROZ TITO

KWAME NKRUMAH

THE NON-ALIGNED NEUTRALITY MOVEMENT BEGAN SOON AFTER THE START OF THE COLD WAR. IT INCLUDED NATIONS THAT, BY AND LARGE, HAD GAINED THEIR INDEPENDENCE FROM VARIOUS EUROPEAN POWERS AFTER WORLD WAR II.

SEEKING STRENGTH THROUGH UNITY, THEY ALSO SOUGHT TO STABILIZE THE CONFLICT BETWEEN THE SUPERPOWERS.

AT THE BANDUNG CONFERENCE IN INDONESIA, 29 ASIAN AND AFRICAN NATIONS PROCLAIMED THEIR OPPOSITION TO INTERFERENCE FROM THE UNITED STATES, SOVIET RUSSIA, OR ANY "IMPERIAL" POWER.

SOME SIGNIFICANT FIGURES AT THE MEETING WERE PRIME MINISTER JAWAHARLAL NEHRU, OF INDIA; PRIME MINISTER GAMAL ABDEL NASSER, OF EGYPT; PRIME MINISTER KWAME NKRUMAH, OF THE GOLD COAST (LATER GHANA); PRESIDENT AHMED SUKARNO, OF INDONESIA; AND PRESIDENT JOSIP BROZ TITO, OF YUGOSLAVIA.

AHMED SUKARNO

GAMAL ABDEL NASSER

GROWING OUT OF THE CONFERENCE AND FORMED IN 1961 WAS THE NON-ALIGNED MOVEMENT, WHOSE MEMBERS WENT ONE STEP FURTHER AND DECLARED NEUTRALITY IN THE SUPERPOWER CONTEST.

OVER THE YEARS, BOTH THE U.S. AND THE SOVIET UNION ATTEMPTED TO BRING THESE NATIONS INTO THEIR RESPECTIVE CAMPS BY SUCH MEANS AS SOVIET FUNDING OF EGYPT'S ASWAN DAM IN THE 1960S AND AMERICA'S AID TO SEVERAL SOUTHEAST ASIAN COUNTRIES.

INCLUDING SUCH COUNTRIES AS INDIA, JAPAN, INDONESIA, YUGOSLAVIA, AND EGYPT, CHE'S TOUR COVERED 14 NATIONS AND RESULTED IN...

...ALMOST NOTHING.

NO NEW TRADE OPENINGS COULD BE ESTABLISHED EXCEPT FOR A SOVIET PROMISE MADE IN CAIRO TO PURCHASE HALF A MILLION TONS OF SUGAR, CUBA'S MAIN EXPORT.

THIS HELPED ENCOURAGE THE LATER CUBAN ALLIANCE.

500,000 TONS USSR

WHEN CHE RETURNED FROM HIS TRIP IN SEPTEMBER, HE LEARNED THAT MUCH HAD OCCURRED AT HOME. THE MODERATES IN CASTRO'S GOVERNMENT WERE BEING PUSHED ASIDE FOR LOYALISTS TO FIDEL.

AN ATTEMPT BY A CUBAN-DOMINICAN GUERRILLA GROUP TO OUST RAFAEL LEÓNIDAS TRUJILLO MOLINA, THE PRESIDENT OF THE DOMINICAN REPUBLIC, WAS IMMEDIATELY DEFEATED.

AND, IN TURN, WHEN AN ARMY PUT TOGETHER BY TRUJILLO ATTEMPTED AN INVASION OF CUBA IN AUGUST, THE INVADERS' TRANSPORT PLANE WAS MET BY WAITING CASTRO FORCES.

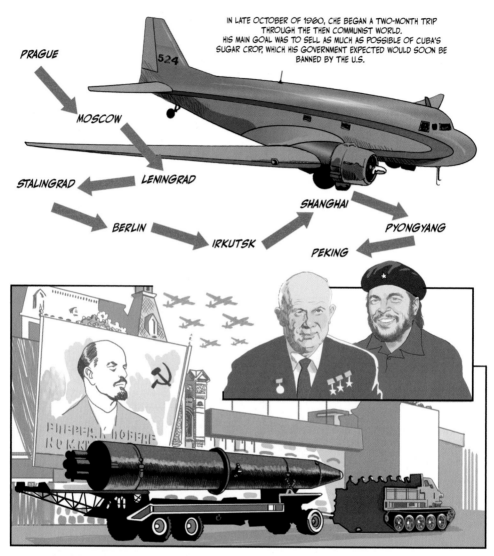

IN LATE OCTOBER OF 1960, CHE BEGAN A TWO-MONTH TRIP THROUGH THE THEN COMMUNIST WORLD.
HIS MAIN GOAL WAS TO SELL AS MUCH AS POSSIBLE OF CUBA'S SUGAR CROP, WHICH HIS GOVERNMENT EXPECTED WOULD SOON BE BANNED BY THE U.S.

PRAGUE

MOSCOW

STALINGRAD

LENINGRAD

BERLIN

IRKUTSK

SHANGHAI

PEKING

PYONGYANG

524

ON NOVEMBER 7, THE 43RD ANNIVERSARY OF THE RUSSIAN REVOLUTION, HE STOOD IN A PLACE OF HONOR BESIDE PREMIER KHRUSHCHEV, VIEWING THE HUGE MILITARY PARADE--WHICH SHOWED THE WORLD CUBA'S GROWING IMPORTANCE IN THE COMMUNIST SPHERE.

JUST AS IMPORTANT, CHE RECEIVED ORDERS FOR SUGAR FROM THE SOVIET UNION AMOUNTING TO 2.7 MILLION TONS.
CHINA ORDERED 1 MILLION TONS.

ON JANUARY 3, 1961, SHORTLY AFTER CHE RETURNED HOME, PRESIDENT EISENHOWER, ACKNOWLEDGING THAT CUBA HAD ENTERED THE COMMUNIST BLOC, ENDED ALL DIPLOMATIC RELATIONS BETWEEN THE TWO NATIONS.

CHAPTER 6: CRISIS AFTER CRISIS

CUBA SUBSEQUENTLY BECAME MORE OPENLY PRO-RUSSIAN. LEARNING ENGLISH WAS DISCOURAGED, WHILE LEARNING RUSSIAN WAS PROMOTED. RUSSIAN TEACHERS AND ADVISERS OF ALL KINDS WERE BROUGHT IN, AND STREET NAMES AND BUSINESSES SOON REFLECTED THE CHANGE.

CHE WAS SAID TO BE A MAJOR CAUSE OF THE CHANGE.

A REPORT OF HIS RECENT TRIP DECLARED, "BY THE END OF HIS VISIT, CUBA HAD TRADE AND PAYMENT AGREEMENTS AND CULTURAL TIES WITH EVERY COUNTRY IN THE [SOVIET] BLOC... AND TECHNICAL ASSISTANCE ACCORDS WITH ALL BUT ALBANIA."

Avenida Lenin ↑

Calle Carlos Marx ↑

Centro Rosa Luxemburg →

Che
COMANDANTE AMIGO

PINAR DEL RIO
HAVANA
MARIEL
MATANZAS
SANTA CLARA
CIENFUEGOS
NUEVITAS
BAYAMO
GUANTANAMO
U.S. NAVAL BASE GUANTANAMO BAY

NEWLY ELECTED PRESIDENT JOHN F. KENNEDY, WHO HAD CRITICIZED EISENHOWER'S CUBAN POLICY AS WEAK, LEARNED THAT THE PREVIOUS ADMINISTRATION HAD PLANNED TO AID AN INVASION BY CUBAN EXPATRIATES...

...WHICH HE NOW HAD TO APPROVE OR ABORT.

THROUGH CUBA'S OWN INFILTRATIONS INSIDE MIAMI'S EXPATRIATE CUBAN COMMUNITY, CASTRO LEARNED MUCH ABOUT THE U.S. PLAN.

WE ATTACK SOON AND WE EXPECT THEIR MILITARY TO AID US.

CASTRO HAD ALSO BEEN SHIPPED LARGE AMOUNTS OF SOVIET ARMS TO BOLSTER HIS DEFENSE. CUBANS WERE READIER THAN EVER TO DEFEND THEMSELVES.

USSR

USSR

ON APRIL 14, 1961, IT STARTED.
EL ENCANTO, THE LARGEST DEPARTMENT STORE
IN HAVANA, WAS SUDDENLY SET AFIRE, ALLEGEDLY BY
CIA-SUPPORTED GROUPS, AND WAS TOTALLY
DESTROYED BY THE FLAMES.

ONE DAY LATER, B-26 INVADER BOMBERS--BEARING
CUBAN COUNTER-REVOLUTIONARY MARKINGS--
BOMBED AND STRAFED THREE DIFFERENT CUBAN
AIRFIELDS, CAUSING GREAT DAMAGE AND ALL BUT
ANNIHILATING THE COUNTRY'S SMALL AIR FORCE.

ON APRIL 17, SHIPS CARRYING 1,500
CUBAN EXILES CAME ASHORE PREDAWN
AT PLAYA GIRÓN, IN THE BAY OF PIGS.

BUT CASTRO'S FORCES WERE FOREWARNED AND READY.
THE LEADER AND HIS TROOPS WERE CAMPED CLOSE TO THE POINT
OF INVASION, WHILE CHE HEADED A GROUP FARTHER AWAY.
THE INVADERS, WHO KENNEDY DECIDED WOULD NOT GET U.S. MILITARY
SUPPORT, WERE MET BY CASTRO'S FORCES WITHIN HOURS.

THREE DAYS LATER, IT WAS OVER.
WITHOUT FURTHER HELP, THE
INVADERS RAN OUT OF SUPPLIES
AND SURRENDERED.

405

TWELVE HUNDRED WERE TAKEN
PRISONER, 114 WERE KILLED,
AND CASTRO'S CUBANS HAD WON
AN IMPORTANT VICTORY.

MONTHS LATER, IN A MEETING WITH KENNEDY
AIDE RICHARD GOODWIN, CHE TOLD HIM...

BLAM!

THANK YOU FOR
PLAYA GIRÓN.

BEFORE THE INVASION
THE REVOLUTION WAS
SHAKY. NOW IT IS
STRONGER THAN EVER.

NEITHER CHE NOR HIS FORCES PARTICIPATED IN THE BATTLE,
BUT HE ALMOST DIED IN A SELF-INFLICTED ACCIDENT.
A PISTOL THAT FELL OUT OF HIS HOLSTER CAUSED A BULLET
TO GRAZE THE SIDE OF HIS FACE, WITHIN INCHES OF HIS BRAIN.

SOON AFTER THE FAILED AMERICAN-BACKED INVASION, THE U.S. CREATED AN ECONOMIC-AID PLAN FOR LATIN AMERICA. CALLED THE ALLIANCE FOR PROGRESS, IT PROMISED $20 BILLION OVER TEN YEARS, AND WAS PRESENTED IN AUGUST 1961 AT AN ORGANIZATION OF AMERICAN STATES CONFERENCE IN URUGUAY.

CHE, IN HIS MILITARY UNIFORM, REPRESENTED CUBA AT THE CONFERENCE.

IN A SPEECH LASTING MORE THAN TWO HOURS, HE CRITICIZED U.S. ACTIONS AGAINST CUBA BUT "GUARANTEED" THAT...

...WE WILL NOT EXPORT REVOLUTIONS.

NOT A SINGLE WEAPON WILL LEAVE CUBA FOR BATTLE IN ANY OTHER COUNTRY IN AMERICA.

ON AUGUST 16, IN HIS CLOSING COMMENTS, HE DECLARED THAT CUBA COULD NOT APPROVE THE ALLIANCE, WHICH HE FELT WAS INTENDED TO ISOLATE IT, BUT THAT HIS NATION WOULD CONFER WITH THE U.S. ...

...ON ANY ISSUE, WITHOUT PRECONDITIONS.

CHE MET KENNEDY'S AIDE RICHARD GOODWIN AT A PARTY ON AUGUST 17, AND GOODWIN LATER REPORTED BACK TO THE PRESIDENT...

ALTHOUGH HE LEFT NO DOUBT OF HIS PERSONAL AND INTENSE DEVOTION TO COMMUNISM, HIS CONVERSATION WAS FREE OF PROPAGANDA AND BOMBAST.

THEY INTEND TO BUILD A SOCIALIST STATE, AND THE REVOLUTION THEY HAVE BEGUN IS IRREVERSIBLE.

THE U.S. TOOK QUICK ACTION AFTER THE CONFERENCE: CHE'S OVERTURE FOR A MEETING WAS TURNED DOWN; CONGRESS BANNED AID TO ANY NATION TRADING WITH CUBA; AND, IN QUICK SUCCESSION, COSTA RICA, VENEZUELA, COLOMBIA, PANAMA, NICARAGUA, EL SALVADOR, AND ARGENTINA ENDED THEIR TRADING TIES WITH CUBA.

BY MARCH 1962, CONDITIONS IN CUBA HAD BECOME SO BAD THAT RATIONING HAD BEGUN. PEOPLE WERE FORCED TO STAND IN LINES TO BUY LIMITED AMOUNTS OF FOOD.

DURING THE FOLLOWING MONTH, SOVIET AGENT ALEXANDER ALEXIEV WAS SUMMONED FROM CUBA TO MEET WITH PREMIER KHRUSHCHEV, WHO TOLD HIM...

...TO SAVE THE CUBAN REVOLUTION, WE HAVE REACHED A DECISION TO PLACE ROCKETS IN CUBA.

THIS WAS THOUGHT TO BE AN ANSWER TO THE U.S. DEPLOYMENT OF NUCLEAR MISSILES IN TURKEY. SURPRISING ALEXIEV, CASTRO ACCEPTED THE OFFER. IN A MEETING WITH HIM AND SEVERAL KEY ADVISERS, CHE DECLARED...

ANYTHING THAT CAN STOP THE AMERICANS IS WORTHWHILE.

HOW WILL FIDEL REACT?

THUS BEGAN WHAT BECAME KNOWN AS *THE CUBAN MISSILE CRISIS.*

BACKGROUND:
THE CUBAN
MISSILE CRISIS

BY THE 1960S, TENSIONS BETWEEN THE U.S. AND THE SOVIET UNION HAD BEGUN TO ESCALATE. SPACE EXPLORATION, THE ARMS RACE, AND COMPETITIVE NUCLEAR TESTS WERE ALL HOT-BUTTON ISSUES.

THE U.S. FUNDED ANTI-COMMUNIST REGIMES IN VIETNAM AND LAOS, AND IN AUGUST OF 1961 THE SOVIETS BUILT A 97-MILE-LONG WALL SEPARATING EAST AND WEST BERLIN.

FIDEL CASTRO'S INCREASING POWER IN CUBA--SHORT MILES FROM U.S. BORDERS--WAS VIEWED AS A GRAVE THREAT BY WASHINGTON. WHEN CUBA ENTERED INTO A TRADE AGREEMENT WITH RUSSIA IN 1960, THE U.S. ENDED ALL TRADE WITH IT AND BEGAN PLOTTING WAYS TO ASSASSINATE OR DEPOSE CASTRO.

THE UTTER FAILURE OF THE AMERICAN-DIRECTED BAY OF PIGS INVASION, MEANT TO TOPPLE FIDEL IN APRIL 1961, WAS AN EMBARRASSMENT. IN SEPTEMBER, THE SOVIETS PUBLICLY PROMISED TO SEND CUBA WEAPONS TO HELP IT DEFEND ITSELF AGAINST ANY FUTURE U.S. THREAT.

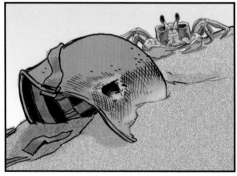

SO WHEN, ON OCTOBER 14, 1962, AN AMERICAN SPY PLANE PHOTOGRAPHED A NUCLEAR-MISSILE SILO BEING BUILT IN CUBA AND PRESIDENT KENNEDY WAS ADVISED THAT IN TEN DAYS CUBA WOULD BE ABLE TO FIRE MISSILES AT AMERICAN TARGETS, HE DECLARED: "WE WILL NOT NEEDLESSLY RISK WORLDWIDE WAR, IN WHICH EVEN VICTORY WOULD BE ASHES IN OUR MOUTH... BUT NEITHER WILL WE SHRINK FROM THAT RISK WHEN IT MUST BE FACED."
NEVER WAS THE WORLD SO CLOSE TO NUCLEAR DISASTER.

RAÚL CASTRO CARRIED THE INITIAL DRAFT OF THE TREATY TO MOSCOW IN EARLY JULY, BUT IT WAS CHE WHO BROUGHT BACK THE REVISED TREATY IN LATE AUGUST.

THERE WILL BE NO PROBLEM FROM THE U.S.

AND IF THERE IS A PROBLEM WE WILL SEND THE BALTIC FLEET.

THE TREATY CALLED FOR INSTALLING 40 NUCLEAR MISSILE LAUNCHERS (ALL UNDER SOVIET COMMAND), 42 MIG INTERCEPTORS, 42 BOMBERS, AND 42,000 SOVIET TROOPS.

ALTHOUGH THE DELIVERY AND PLACEMENT OF ALL MATERIAL WAS DONE IN GREAT SECRECY, BY EARLY SEPTEMBER THE U.S. ADMINISTRATION HAD UNCOVERED MUCH OF THE STORY.

U-2 FLIGHTS PHOTOGRAPHED MISSILE SITES AND INSTALLATIONS.

RECONNAISSANCE PHOTOS SUGGEST THAT THE SOVIETS ARE BUILDING A SUB BASE.

THOUGH "ASSURED" BY SOVIET AMBASSADOR ANATOLY DOBRYNIN THAT THEY WERE DELIVERING ONLY DEFENSIVE WEAPONS TO CUBA, PRESIDENT KENNEDY TOLD CONGRESS...

UNITED STATES CONGRESS

...I AM ASKING YOU TO CALL UP 150,000 RESERVISTS.

AND ON OCTOBER 6, 1962, THE PRESIDENT WAS SHOWN A U-2 FLIGHT PHOTO THAT REVEALED THE BUILDING OF AN SS-4 SITE AT SAN CRISTÓBAL, CUBA.

MRBM LAUNCH SITE 2 SAN CRISTÓBAL

TELL FOREIGN MINISTER GROMYKO I WANT TO SEE HIM.

TWO DAYS LATER, KENNEDY MET WITH GROMYKO, WHO CLAIMED THAT NO OFFENSIVE WEAPONS HAD BEEN GIVEN TO CUBA. HIS COUNTRY WAS INVOLVED ONLY IN LAND REFORMS AND DEFENSE, HE SAID.

ON OCTOBER 22, KENNEDY ANNOUNCED TO THE AMERICAN PEOPLE THAT THE U.S. WOULD...

...REGARD ANY NUCLEAR MISSILE LAUNCHED FROM CUBA AGAINST ANY NATION IN THE WESTERN HEMISPHERE...AS AN ATTACK ON THE U.S. REQUIRING FULL RETALIATORY RESPONSE.

A NAVAL "QUARANTINE" WAS ALSO PLACED ON CUBA TO PREVENT ANY FURTHER MILITARY SHIPMENTS.

U.S.A.

QUARANTINE INTERDICTION LINE

13 DESTROYERS

CUBA

ON OCTOBER 24, 13 SOVIET SHIPS HEADING FOR CUBA MET THE U.S. "QUARANTINE" AND SUDDENLY DISCONTINUED THEIR COURSE. AT THAT TIME, SECRETARY OF STATE DEAN RUSK FAMOUSLY TOLD NATIONAL SECURITY ADVISER MCGEORGE BUNDY...

WE'RE EYEBALL TO EYEBALL, AND I THINK THE OTHER FELLOW JUST BLINKED.

HOWEVER, THE CRISIS WAS FAR FROM OVER. DAYS FOLLOWED WITH THREATS AND COUNTER-THREATS AS THE U.S. AND THE SOVIET UNION STOOD ON THE BRINK OF WAR.

70

73

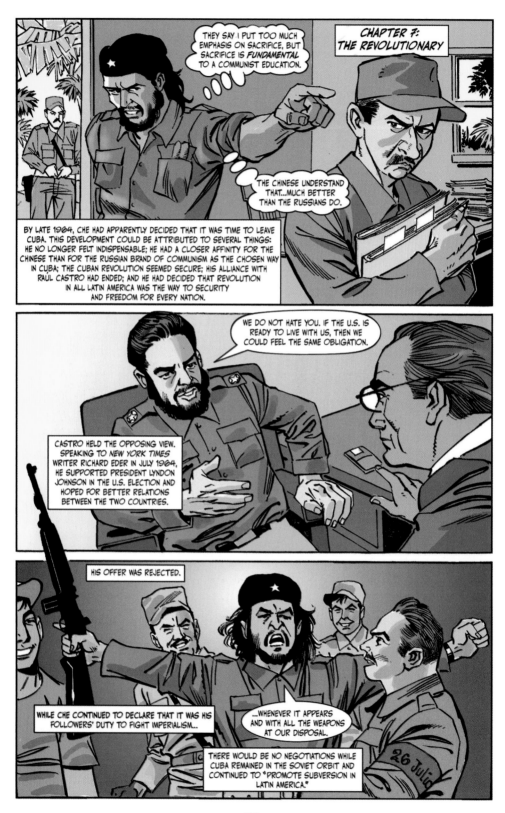

THEY SAY I PUT TOO MUCH EMPHASIS ON SACRIFICE, BUT SACRIFICE IS *FUNDAMENTAL* TO A COMMUNIST EDUCATION.

THE CHINESE UNDERSTAND THAT...MUCH BETTER THAN THE RUSSIANS DO.

CHAPTER 7:
THE REVOLUTIONARY

BY LATE 1964, CHE HAD APPARENTLY DECIDED THAT IT WAS TIME TO LEAVE CUBA. THIS DEVELOPMENT COULD BE ATTRIBUTED TO SEVERAL THINGS: HE NO LONGER FELT INDISPENSABLE; HE HAD A CLOSER AFFINITY FOR THE CHINESE THAN FOR THE RUSSIAN BRAND OF COMMUNISM AS THE CHOSEN WAY IN CUBA; THE CUBAN REVOLUTION SEEMED SECURE; HIS ALLIANCE WITH RAÚL CASTRO HAD ENDED; AND HE HAD DECIDED THAT REVOLUTION IN ALL LATIN AMERICA WAS THE WAY TO SECURITY AND FREEDOM FOR EVERY NATION.

WE DO NOT HATE YOU. IF THE U.S. IS READY TO LIVE WITH US, THEN WE COULD FEEL THE SAME OBLIGATION.

CASTRO HELD THE OPPOSING VIEW. SPEAKING TO *NEW YORK TIMES* WRITER RICHARD EDER IN JULY 1964, HE SUPPORTED PRESIDENT LYNDON JOHNSON IN THE U.S. ELECTION AND HOPED FOR BETTER RELATIONS BETWEEN THE TWO COUNTRIES.

HIS OFFER WAS REJECTED.

WHILE CHE CONTINUED TO DECLARE THAT IT WAS HIS FOLLOWERS' DUTY TO FIGHT IMPERIALISM...

...WHENEVER IT APPEARS AND WITH ALL THE WEAPONS AT OUR DISPOSAL.

THERE WOULD BE NO NEGOTIATIONS WHILE CUBA REMAINED IN THE SOVIET ORBIT AND CONTINUED TO "PROMOTE SUBVERSION IN LATIN AMERICA."

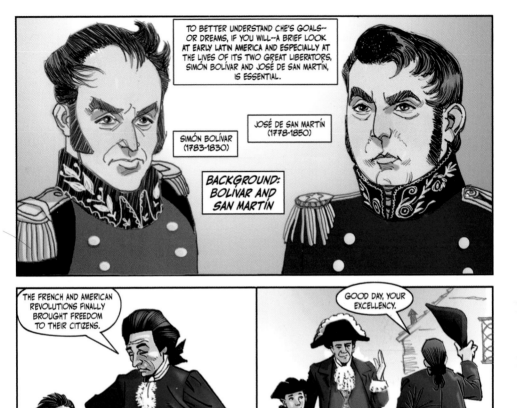

TO BETTER UNDERSTAND CHE'S GOALS-- OR DREAMS, IF YOU WILL--A BRIEF LOOK AT EARLY LATIN AMERICA AND ESPECIALLY AT THE LIVES OF ITS TWO GREAT LIBERATORS, SIMÓN BOLÍVAR AND JOSÉ DE SAN MARTÍN, IS ESSENTIAL.

JOSÉ DE SAN MARTÍN (1778-1850)

SIMÓN BOLÍVAR (1783-1830)

BACKGROUND: BOLÍVAR AND SAN MARTÍN

THE FRENCH AND AMERICAN REVOLUTIONS FINALLY BROUGHT FREEDOM TO THEIR CITIZENS.

GOOD DAY, YOUR EXCELLENCY.

SAN MARTÍN WAS BORN ON FEBRUARY 25, 1778, IN YAPEYO, IN THE ARGENTINE PROVINCE OF CORRIENTES. HE ALSO CAME FROM WEALTH, HIS FATHER BEING THE GOVERNOR OF THE PROVINCE.

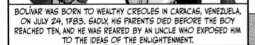

BOLÍVAR WAS BORN TO WEALTHY CREOLES IN CARACAS, VENEZUELA, ON JULY 24, 1783. SADLY, HIS PARENTS DIED BEFORE THE BOY REACHED TEN, AND HE WAS REARED BY AN UNCLE WHO EXPOSED HIM TO THE IDEAS OF THE ENLIGHTENMENT.

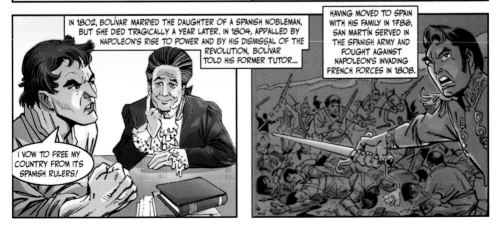

IN 1802, BOLÍVAR MARRIED THE DAUGHTER OF A SPANISH NOBLEMAN, BUT SHE DIED TRAGICALLY A YEAR LATER. IN 1804, APPALLED BY NAPOLEON'S RISE TO POWER AND BY HIS DISMISSAL OF THE REVOLUTION, BOLÍVAR TOLD HIS FORMER TUTOR...

HAVING MOVED TO SPAIN WITH HIS FAMILY IN 1786, SAN MARTÍN SERVED IN THE SPANISH ARMY AND FOUGHT AGAINST NAPOLEON'S INVADING FRENCH FORCES IN 1808.

I VOW TO FREE MY COUNTRY FROM ITS SPANISH RULERS!

BACK IN VENEZUELA, BOLÍVAR SPOKE BEFORE THE NATIONAL CONGRESS IN CARACAS IN 1811.

LET US LAY THE CORNERSTONE OF AMERICAN FREEDOM WITHOUT FEAR. TO HESITATE IS TO PERISH.

THE FIRST REPUBLIC WAS DECLARED ON JULY 5 OF THAT YEAR, VENEZUELA BECOMING THE FIRST COLONY IN THE SPANISH EMPIRE TO GAIN ITS FREEDOM.

RESIGNING FROM THE SPANISH ARMY THAT SAME YEAR, SAN MARTÍN RETURNED TO BUENOS AIRES, WHERE HE RETAINED HIS LIEUTENANT-COLONEL RANK AND FORMED THE FAMED CAVALRY REGIMENT, THE MOUNTED GRENADIERS.

CHARGE!

BOLÍVAR ALSO JOINED THE LAUTARO LODGE, WHICH PLEDGED TO LIBERATE SOUTH AMERICA FROM SPANISH RULE.

HOWEVER, THE ARMIES UNDER THE COMMAND OF FRANCISCO DE MIRANDA-- WITH BOLÍVAR SERVING AS A LIEUTENANT COLONEL--WERE INEXPERIENCED.

A DEADLY EARTHQUAKE IN 1812 HELPED THE SPANIARDS REGAIN CONTROL. BOLÍVAR FLED TO NEW GRANADA (NOW COLOMBIA).

IN SAN MARTÍN'S FIRST SOUTH AMERICAN ENCOUNTER, IN 1813, HIS ARMIES DEFEATED A ROYALIST FORCE. BUT WHEN HE WAS SENT TO FIGHT IN THE NORTHERN PROVINCES OF ARGENTINA, HE BECAME VERY ILL AND WAS FORCED TO RETIRE.

76

DURING THE ENSUING YEAR, VARIOUS BATTLES TOOK PLACE THAT FAVORED ONE SIDE AND THEN THE OTHER. FINALLY, IN 1819, BOLÍVAR LED A LARGE FORCE THROUGH THE ANDES THAT SPLIT THE SPANISH TROOPS AND DEFEATED THEM.

HE WAS THEN ELECTED PRESIDENT OF GREATER COLOMBIA (TODAY COLOMBIA, VENEZUELA, ECUADOR, AND PANAMA).

IN 1817, SAN MARTÍN LED AN ARMY OF 3,250 MEN OVER THE 15,000-FOOT-HIGH ANDES--A FEAT COMPARED TO HANNIBAL'S CROSSING OF THE ALPS-- AND DEFEATED THE SPANISH FORCES IN CHILE.

THEN, IN 1821, IN A SURPRISE STRIKE BY SEA, HE CAPTURED LIMA AND WAS DECLARED THE PROTECTOR OF PERU.

IN JULY OF 1822, BOLÍVAR AND SAN MARTÍN HELD A SECRET MEETING IN GUAYAQUIL, ECUADOR. WHAT WAS DISCUSSED IS STILL UNKNOWN, BUT SAN MARTÍN SOON RESIGNED HIS POSITIONS AND RETIRED FROM PUBLIC LIFE, FLEEING TO EUROPE. BOLÍVAR WENT ON TO TAKE OVER PERU AND BOLIVIA AND TO ORGANIZE THE GOVERNMENTS OF THE TWO COUNTRIES.

THOUGH THIS UNION SOON FELL APART, IT WAS THE BEGINNING OF PAN-AMERICANISM AND CERTAINLY AN INSPIRATION FOR CHE GUEVARA.

IN LATE 1964, THE URUGUAYAN JOURNALIST EDUARDO HUGHES GALEANO DESCRIBED CHE IN THIS MANNER...

CHE WAS NOT A DESK MAN. HE WAS A CREATOR OF REVOLUTIONS, AND IT WAS APPARENT THAT HE WAS NOT...AN ADMINISTRATOR.

SOMEHOW THAT TENSION OF A CAGED LION THAT HIS APPARENT CALM BETRAYED HAD TO EXPLODE.

THAT YEAR, THIS "CREATOR OF REVOLUTIONS" STARTED MOVING ABOUT THE GLOBE, AS IF SEEKING THE PLACE IN WHICH TO BEGIN. IN NOVEMBER, HE REPRESENTED CUBA IN MOSCOW AT THE 47TH ANNIVERSARY OF THE BOLSHEVIK REVOLUTION.

HE MET WITH MANY REPRESENTATIVES OF THE NEW SOVIET GOVERNMENT, NOW HEADED BY LEONID BREZHNEV. ONE OF THEM, VITALI KORIONOV, DEPUTY CHIEF OF THE CENTRAL COMMITTEE'S AMERICAS DEPARTMENT, SAID...

CHE COULD SEE FOR HIMSELF WHAT WAS GOING ON.

A NEW REVOLUTION IN LATIN AMERICA--RE-CREATING THE ONE PURSUED BY BOLÍVAR AND SAN MARTÍN, BUT THIS TIME LED BY MARXIST PARTIES--WAS NOT SUPPORTED BY RUSSIA.

RETURNING TO CUBA, CHE CONTINUED TO CHAMPION REVOLUTION.

SPEAKING IN SANTIAGO ON NOVEMBER 30, 1964, AND REFERRING TO AMERICAN SUPPORT OF BELGIUM'S MILITARY INTERVENTION IN THE CONGO, SUPRESSING COMMUNIST REBELS, HE RANTED...

JUST AS THE HITLERIAN HORDES WERE BEASTS, SO ARE THE AMERICANS AND BELGIAN PARATROOPERS BEASTS... BECAUSE IT IS THE VERY NATURE OF IMPERIALISM WHICH BESTIALIZES MEN, WHICH CONVERTS THEM INTO WILD ANIMALS WILLING TO SLIT THROATS, COMMIT MURDER, AND DESTROY.

SOON AFTERWARD, IN DECEMBER, HE FLEW TO NEW YORK TO REPRESENT CUBA AT THE U.N. GENERAL ASSEMBLY. ONCE AGAIN, REFERRING TO EVENTS IN THE CONGO, HE WENT ON...
"HOW CAN THE U.S., WHICH MURDERS ITS OWN CHILDREN AND DISCRIMINATES BETWEEN THEM DAILY BECAUSE OF THE COLOR OF THEIR SKIN, WHICH ALLOWS THE MURDERERS OF NEGROES TO GO FREE...CLAIM TO BE THE GUARDIAN OF LIBERTY?"

ONE AMERICAN WHO APPLAUDED CHE'S COMMENTS WAS MALCOLM X. ON DECEMBER 13, TWO MONTHS BEFORE HIS ASSASSINATION, MALCOLM X TOLD AN AUDIENCE THAT HAD JUST APPLAUDED THE MENTION OF CHE'S NAME...

I'M HAPPY TO HEAR YOUR WARM ROUND OF APPLAUSE... BECAUSE IT LETS THE MAN KNOW THAT HE'S JUST NOT IN A POSITION TO TELL US WHO WE SHOULD APPLAUD FOR AND WHO WE SHOULDN'T APPLAUD FOR.

AND YOU DON'T SEE ANY ANTI-CASTRO CUBANS HERE--WE EAT THEM UP.

80

ACTING AS CASTRO'S AMBASSADOR, CHE LEFT NEW YORK IN MID-DECEMBER. DURING THE NEXT TWO MONTHS, HE ROAMED AFRICA, MEETING WITH, AMONG OTHERS,...

AGOSTINHO NETO OF ANGOLA

ALPHONSE MASSAMBA-DEBAT OF CONGO

PRIME MINISTER KWAME NKRUMAH OF GHANA

AFRICA'S LIBERATION FROM ITS COLONIAL MASTERS!

STANDING WITH VIETNAM AGAINST THE AMERICAN IMPERIALISTS!

IN AN INTERVIEW WITH THE MAGAZINE *RÉVOLUTION AFRICAINE*, CHE SAID THAT AFRICA WAS ONE OF...

AHMED BEN BELLA ALGERIA

...THE IMPORTANT FIELDS OF STRUGGLE AGAINST ALL FORMS OF EXPLOITATION EXISTING IN THE WORLD...

...AGAINST IMPERIALISM, COLONIALISM, AND NEOCOLONIALISM.

UNITY OF ALL ANTI-COLONIAL NATIONS!

ON FEBRUARY 25, 1965, CHE GAVE HIS LAST SPEECH IN AFRICA, APPEARING BEFORE MORE THAN 40 AFRICAN AND ASIAN DELEGATIONS FROM THIRD WORLD COUNTRIES, AND GUERRILLA GROUPS. THIS WOULD BE HIS LAST PUBLIC ADDRESS.

IN WHAT SEEMED AN ATTACK ON THE SOVIET UNION, HE DECLARED, "THE DEVELOPMENT OF COUNTRIES THAT NOW BEGIN THE ROAD TO LIBERATION MUST BE UNDERWRITTEN BY THE SOCIALIST COUNTRIES...

...HOW CAN MUTUAL BENEFIT MEAN SELLING AT WORLD-MARKET PRICES RAW MATERIALS THAT COST UNLIMITED SWEAT AND SUFFERING TO THE BACKWARD COUNTRIES...

ANC

OAU

...AND BUYING AT WORLD-MARKET PRICES THE MACHINES PRODUCED IN THE LARGE AUTOMATED FACTORIES OF TODAY?"

THE SOCIALIST COUNTRIES HAVE A MORAL DUTY TO LIQUIDATE THEIR TACIT COMPLICITY WITH THE WEST...

...WITHOUT ANY COST WHATSOEVER AND IN QUANTITIES DETERMINED BY THEIR NEED AND AVAILABILITY TO THOSE PEOPLE WHO ASK FOR THEM.

HE CONCLUDED BY SAYING THAT WEAPONS FROM THESE SOCIALIST NATIONS SHOULD BE DONATED...

CHE'S COMMENTS INFURIATED SOVIET RUSSIA.

WHEN CHE RETURNED TO CUBA ON MARCH 15, FIDEL CASTRO WAS AMONG THOSE WHO GREETED HIM AT THE AIRPORT.

THEN THE TWO MEN SUPPOSEDLY WENT INTO A CLOSED-DOOR MEETING THAT LASTED FOR HOURS.

WHAT WAS DISCUSSED REMAINS UNKNOWN.

BUT LITTLE MORE THAN TWO WEEKS LATER, ON APRIL 1, CHE TOOK OFF FOR AFRICA DISGUISED AS A QUIET, CLEAN-SHAVEN, BESPECTACLED GENTLEMAN NAMED RAMÓN BENITEZ...

...HAVING BEEN INSTRUCTED BY CASTRO TO LEAD A BRIGADE OF CUBAN GUERRILLAS WHO HAD BEEN TRAINING IN THE CONGO.

AFTER A LABYRINTHINE JOURNEY BY WAY OF MOSCOW AND CAIRO, A DISGUISED CHE LANDED IN THE TANZANIAN PORT CITY OF DAR ES SALAAM ON APRIL 19, 1965. HE HAD TRAVELED WITH PAPI TAMAYO, HIS FRIEND AND EMISSARY, AND VICTOR DREKE, A BLACK COMMANDER OF THE CUBAN BRIGADE AND CHE'S SECOND IN COMMAND.

"NOBODY KNEW ME," CHE WROTE LATER. "NOT EVEN THE VERY AMBASSADOR, AN OLD COMRADE-IN-ARMS."

CHAPTER 8: THE CONGO MISADVENTURE

CHE LATER WROTE...

I HAD LEFT BEHIND ALMOST ELEVEN YEARS OF WORK FOR THE CUBAN REVOLUTION AT FIDEL'S SIDE, A HAPPY HOME...AND A BUNCH OF KIDS* WHO BARELY KNEW MY LOVE.

*FOUR.

THE CUBAN AMBASSADOR PABLO RIBALTA HAD THE MEN HOUSED ON A SMALL FARM ON THE OUTSKIRTS OF THE CITY, WHERE THEY AWAITED THE ARRIVAL OF THE MEMBERS OF THE CUBAN BRIGADE.

CHE WOULD BE FIGHTING WITH THE PRO-LUMUMBA MARXIST REBELS AGAINST THE REGULAR CONGOLESE ARMY AND A MERCENARY FORCE HEADED BY MIKE HOARE, A FAMED IRISH SOLDIER-FOR-HIRE.

THEN KNOWN AS "TATO" ("THREE" IN SWAHILI), THE WHITE CHE WAS INTRODUCED TO BLACK GUERRILLAS AS A DOCTOR WHO SPOKE FRENCH AND WAS A VETERAN OF GUERRILLA WARFARE.

"TATO" SOON INFORMED ONE OF HIS CONTACTS...

WE EXPECT TO HAVE A CONTINGENT OF ABOUT 130 MEN, AND WOULD HOPE TO ENTER [THE CONGO] AS QUICKLY AS IT CAN BE ARRANGED.

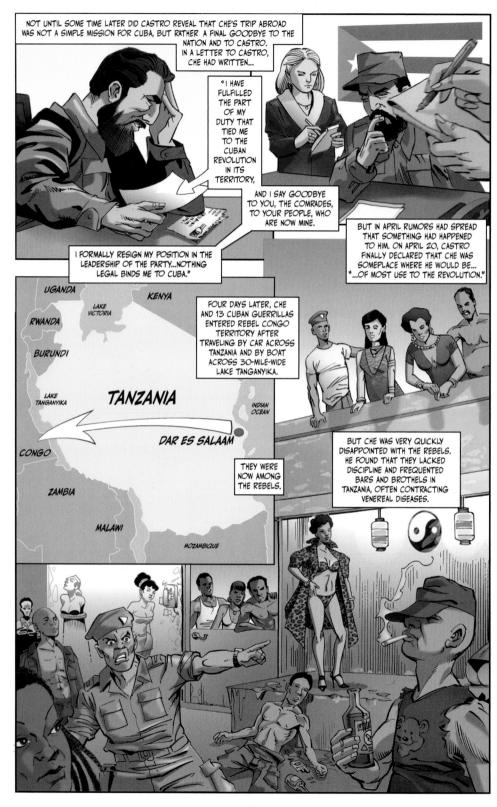

NOT UNTIL SOME TIME LATER DID CASTRO REVEAL THAT CHE'S TRIP ABROAD WAS NOT A SIMPLE MISSION FOR CUBA, BUT RATHER A FINAL GOODBYE TO THE NATION AND TO CASTRO. IN A LETTER TO CASTRO, CHE HAD WRITTEN...

"I HAVE FULFILLED THE PART OF MY DUTY THAT TIED ME TO THE CUBAN REVOLUTION IN ITS TERRITORY,

AND I SAY GOODBYE TO YOU, THE COMRADES, TO YOUR PEOPLE, WHO ARE NOW MINE.

I FORMALLY RESIGN MY POSITION IN THE LEADERSHIP OF THE PARTY...NOTHING LEGAL BINDS ME TO CUBA."

BUT IN APRIL RUMORS HAD SPREAD THAT SOMETHING HAD HAPPENED TO HIM. ON APRIL 20, CASTRO FINALLY DECLARED THAT CHE WAS SOMEPLACE WHERE HE WOULD BE... "...OF MOST USE TO THE REVOLUTION."

FOUR DAYS LATER, CHE AND 13 CUBAN GUERRILLAS ENTERED REBEL CONGO TERRITORY AFTER TRAVELING BY CAR ACROSS TANZANIA AND BY BOAT ACROSS 30-MILE-WIDE LAKE TANGANYIKA.

UGANDA
KENYA
LAKE VICTORIA
RWANDA
BURUNDI
LAKE TANGANYIKA
TANZANIA
INDIAN OCEAN
CONGO
DAR ES SALAAM
ZAMBIA
MALAWI
MOZAMBIQUE

THEY WERE NOW AMONG THE REBELS.

BUT CHE WAS VERY QUICKLY DISAPPOINTED WITH THE REBELS. HE FOUND THAT THEY LACKED DISCIPLINE AND FREQUENTED BARS AND BROTHELS IN TANZANIA, OFTEN CONTRACTING VENEREAL DISEASES.

84

THEY ALSO FOLLOWED *DAWA*, A FORM OF WITCHCRAFT, AND BELIEVED A CERTAIN POTION PROTECTED THEM FROM HARM.

THE ENEMY PLANES ARE NOT IMPORTANT. WITH THIS POTION THEIR BULLETS CANNOT HARM US.

AND, AS CHE WROTE, BECAUSE OF THEIR LIMITED KNOWLEDGE OF FIREARMS, "THEY SHOT THEMSELVES BY PLAYING WITH THEM OR BY CARELESSNESS."

BLAM!

AAHHH!

NO ONE MUST KNOW, *PLEASE*, NO ONE MUST KNOW!

IT WOULD BE AN INTERNATIONAL SCANDAL!

STILL IN DISGUISE, CHE FINALLY DISCLOSED HIS IDENTITY TO GODEFROIO CHAMALESO, A CONGOLESE REPRESENTATIVE. THE REACTION WAS DEVASTATING.

ALL OF CHE'S SUGGESTIONS TO PUT HIS MEN INTO ACTION WERE REJECTED OR COMPLETELY EVADED. AS CHE REMEMBERED...

"ALREADY MURMURS WERE BEGINNING AMONG THE COMRADES ABOUT HOW THE DAYS WERE FRUITLESSLY SLIPPING BY."

IN ADDITION, HIS MEN SUFFERED FROM THE SIDE EFFECTS OF THE ANTI-MALARIAL TABLETS, INCLUDING WEAKNESS, APATHY, AND, ACCORDING TO CHE, "INCIPIENT PESSIMISM."

FINALLY, IN EARLY MAY, CHE WAS GIVEN APPROVAL TO MOVE HIS MEN TO THE UPPER BASE OF LUALABORG MOUNTAIN. THIS BECAME A FOUR-HOUR TREK TO THIS 8,000-FOOT-HIGH OUTPOST.

WITHIN DAYS, CHE BECAME SERIOUSLY ILL, WITH A VERY HIGH FEVER AND A FRIGHTENING CASE OF DELIRIUM. THE EFFECTS LASTED FOR A MONTH, AND 10 OF HIS 30 MEN WERE SIMILARLY AFFLICTED.

BOTH GOOD AND BAD NEWS CAME ON MAY 22. THE GOOD NEWS WAS THAT 17 CUBAN FIGHTERS APPEARED IN CAMP, LED BY OSMANY CIENFUEGOS, AND 17 MORE WERE DUE TO CROSS THE LAKE FROM TANZANIA.

THE BAD NEWS, ACCORDING TO CHE, WAS "THE SADDEST NEWS OF THE WAR." HE WAS INFORMED...

YOUR MOTHER IS VERY SICK, CHE.

A MONTH LATER, HE LEARNED THAT SHE HAD DIED.

CELIA HAD DIED MAY 19, FROM CANCER, AT THE AGE OF 58. AT THE FUNERAL SERVICE, CHE'S PHOTOGRAPH SAT ATOP HER COFFIN. AS IF "CELIA ONLY HAD ONE CHILD," RECALLED HER DAUGHTER-IN-LAW MARIA ELENA DUARTE.

ON JUNE 29, THE CUBAN FORCE WAS FINALLY PUT INTO ACTION. ALTHOUGH CHE WAS NOT ALLOWED TO TAKE PART IN THE ATTACK, 40 CUBANS FOUGHT ALONGSIDE 160 CONGOLESE AND RWANDAN TUTSIS IN THE ASSAULT ON THE ENCAMPMENT AT FORT BANDERA.

IT WAS A COMPLETE DISASTER.

MANY FLED, MANY ABANDONED THEIR WEAPONS, MANY REFUSED TO FIGHT...

...AND ONE OF THE CUBANS LOST HIS DIARY ON THE BATTLEFIELD.

THE CIA THEN KNEW THAT CUBA WAS AIDING THE CONGOLESE REBELS.

THIS BATTLE TYPIFIED THE INEFFICIENCY AND INEPTITUDE OF THE REBEL TROOPS.

ON AUGUST 12, CHE TOLD HIS CUBAN GUERRILLAS...

WINNING A WAR WITH SUCH TROOPS IS OUT OF THE QUESTION.

BECAUSE OF THE POOR SHOWING OF THEIR CONGOLESE COMRADES, MANY OF CHE'S CUBAN TROOPS--BOTH FIGHTERS AND DOCTORS--LEFT THEIR UNITS AND RETURNED HOME.

STILL, CASTRO CONTINUED TO SEND NEW CONTINGENTS OF CUBAN GUERRILLAS INTO THE CONGO BY WAY OF TANZANIA. ANOTHER GROUP, INCLUDING TWO OF CHE'S COMRADES, ARRIVED IN SEPTEMBER.

BUT NOTHING WOULD MAKE UP FOR THE INADEQUACY OF THE CONGOLESE REBELS. WHEN THEY REFUSED TO FOLLOW HIS ORDERS ONE DAY, CHE EXCLAIMED...

I'D PREFER TO HAVE AN ARMY OF *WOMEN* RATHER THAN MEN LIKE YOU!

THE REBELS RESPONDED BY LAUGHING.

THE EXPECTED OFFENSIVE BY GOVERNMENT SOLDIERS AND HOARE'S MERCENARIES BEGAN IN OCTOBER. AIDED BY GUNBOATS, BOMBERS, AND HELICOPTERS, THE COMBINED ARMIES HIT THE GUERRILLAS ON THREE FRONTS ATTEMPTING TO ENCIRCLE THEM.

THE REBEL FORCES COLLAPSED QUICKLY AND CONGOLESE AS WELL AS CUBANS RACED TOWARD LAKE TANGANYIKA AND SAFETY.

IN MID-OCTOBER, A POLITICAL SETTLEMENT WAS REACHED BETWEEN THE CONGOLESE GOVERNMENT AND THE ORGANIZATION OF AFRICAN UNITY (OAU), SUPPORTERS OF THE REBELS. CONGOLESE PRIME MINISTER MOISE TSHOMBE--WHO HAD ENLISTED BELGIAN AND MERCENARY FORCES--WAS TO BE DEPOSED AND ALL FOREIGN FORCES, INCLUDING THE CUBANS, WERE TO LEAVE.

CAUGHT SOMEWHAT BY SURPRISE, CHE'S CAMP WAS CAPTURED BY GOVERNMENT TROOPS ON OCTOBER 24. HUTS WERE BURNED DOWN BY THE CUBAN REBELS, BUT IN THE HURRIED RETREAT CACHES OF ARMAMENTS WERE LEFT BEHIND.

CHE TOOK RESPONSIBILITY FOR MANY OF THE FAILURES, INCLUDING THE DEATHS OF SIX CUBANS. HE LATER WROTE...

PERSONALLY, MY MORALE WAS TERRIBLY DEPRESSED; I FELT RESPONSIBLE FOR THAT DISASTER THROUGH WEAKNESS AND LACK OF FORESIGHT.

AT THAT JUNCTURE, CHE STILL HELD OUT HOPE.

LEAVING A MAN BEHIND TO CONTINUE TRAINING THE REBELS, HE WENT TO THE LAKE CITY OF KIBAMBA TO MEET WITH CONGOLESE REBEL LEADERS.

90

BUT CHE'S HOPES QUICKLY COOLED. BECAUSE OF THE AGREEMENT WITH THE OAU, TANZANIA ENDED ITS ASSOCIATION WITH THE CONGOLESE REBELS ON NOVEMBER 1. CHE WROTE TO CASTRO...

"IT WAS THE COUP DE GRÂCE FOR A MORIBUND REVOLUTION."

CHE STILL SOUGHT SOME KIND OF SUPPORT FROM TANZANIA, EVEN AS REBEL POSITION AFTER REBEL POSITION WAS OVERRUN.

THE SCENE AT LAKE TANGANYIKA WAS TRAGIC. BECAUSE SPACE ON THE BOAT WAS LIMITED, SOME REBELS HAD TO BE LEFT BEHIND, LIKELY TO FACE ONCOMING GOVERNMENT TROOPS.

BY NOVEMBER 20, ANY RESISTANCE SEEMED FOOLHARDY. CHE ORDERED HIS CONTINGENT OF 200 MEN TO DESTROY THEIR HUTS, BURY THEIR WEAPONS AND EQUIPMENT, AND HURRY TO THE LAKE FOR TRANSPORT.

"I HAD TO REJECT MEN WHO PLEADED TO BE TAKEN ALONG. THERE WAS NOT A TRACE OF GRANDEUR IN THIS RETREAT, NOR A GESTURE OF REBELLION."

91

THE LAKE CROSSING PROVED DANGEROUS, THE BOATS WERE THREATENED BY A GOVERNMENT CUTTER. CHE ORDERED THE MEN TO MOUNT RIFLES ON THE BOAT, WHICH SEEMED TO KEEP THE CUTTER AT BAY.

ONCE SAFELY BACK IN TANZANIA, CHE SPOKE TO HIS THREE CLOSEST COMPANIONS.

ARE YOU READY TO CONTINUE?

WHERE?

WHEREVER.

BUT CHE WAS LEFT ALONE. HE HAD NO PLACE TO GO.

ALL THE CUBANS BUT CHE WERE THEN FLOWN ON A SOVIET AIRCRAFT TO MOSCOW, THEN ON A CUBAN AIRCRAFT BACK HOME.

CHE WAS HIDDEN AT THE RESIDENCE OF THE CUBAN EMBASSY AT DAR ES SALAAM, IN A TWO-ROOM APARTMENT WHERE HE STAYED FOR MONTHS.

ON NOVEMBER 25, JOSEPH MOBUTU, CHIEF OF STAFF OF THE CONGOLESE ARMY, LED A SUCCESSFUL COUP THAT OUSTED PRESIDENT JOSEPH KASAVUBU. MOBUTU'S ABSOLUTE RULE WOULD LAST FOR YEARS.

THE REVOLUTION IN THE CONGO WAS OVER.

WHILE CHE WAS BEING SHELTERED IN THE CUBAN EMBASSY, HE WROTE ABOUT THE REVOLUTION, WHICH WAS "A STORY OF FAILURE."

"I HAVE COME OUT WITH MORE FAITH IN THE GUERRILLA STRUGGLE, BUT WE HAVE FAILED. MY RESPONSIBILITY IS GREAT. I WILL NOT FORGET THE DEFEAT, NOR ITS MOST PRECIOUS LESSONS."

CHE ALSO REQUESTED AND RECEIVED A VISIT FROM HIS WIFE, ALEIDA, WHO ARRIVED IN JANUARY AND REMAINED FOR SIX WEEKS.

FINALLY, IN MARCH, CHE LEFT HIS RETREAT IN TANZANIA AND FLEW TO PRAGUE, WHERE HE WOULD DECIDE HIS NEXT DESTINATION.

ACCORDING TO CHE'S WIFE, ALEIDA...

CHE WAS BROUGHT TO PRAGUE AS JUST ANOTHER LATIN AMERICAN REVOLUTIONARY UNDER A FALSE IDENTITY. THE CZECHS NEVER KNEW HE WAS THERE.

AND CHE WAS PLACED IN A "SAFE HOUSE" ON THE OUTSKIRTS OF THE CITY.

ALEIDA AGAIN JOINED HIM IN A FOREIGN COUNTRY, STAYING FOR SEVERAL WEEKS.

DURING THE FOLLOWING MONTHS, CHE AND HIS ASSOCIATES DISCUSSED HIS NEXT DESTINATION. IT WOULD BE SOMEWHERE IN SOUTH AMERICA. BUT WHERE?

PERU?

COLOMBIA?

VENEZUELA?

GUATEMALA?

BOLIVIA?

BECAUSE OF THE STRENGTH OF THE COMMUNIST PARTY WITHIN CERTAIN COUNTRIES, FIVE NATIONS WERE THE MORE OBVIOUS CHOICES.

94

ONE POPULAR CHOICE, HOWEVER, WAS QUICKLY ELIMINATED. IN GUATEMALA, COMMUNIST PARTY HEADQUARTERS WAS INVADED BY THE NATION'S SECURITY FORCES, WHO SEIZED MORE THAN 20 MAJOR OFFICIALS AND THEN KILLED THEM.

BUT ACCORDING TO CHE'S WIFE, ALEIDA...

"ONE OF THE WAYS WE CONVINCED [CHE] TO COME TO PRAGUE WAS BY GETTING HIM ENTHUSIASTIC ABOUT THE POSSIBILITIES IN BOLIVIA...

...FIRST BECAUSE OF ITS PROXIMITY TO ARGENTINA, WHICH WAS VERY IMPORTANT TO CHE. NEXT...THE HUMAN ASSETS AND THE PARTY'S MILITANT TRADITIONS.

AND, FINALLY, BECAUSE OF ITS GEOGRAPHICAL LOCATION, WHICH OFFERED GOOD POSSIBILITIES FOR THE LATER DISPERSION OF GUERRILLAS... TO THE NEIGHBORING COUNTRIES."

...AND, SECRETED IN HAVANA, HE BEGAN MAKING PREPARATIONS FOR A REVOLUTION IN BOLIVIA.

CHE ARRIVED BACK IN CUBA IN LATE JULY 1966.

ONE MONTH LATER, THE SELECTED MEMBERS OF A CUBAN GUERRILLA FORCE--ABOUT 150 MEN--CAME TOGETHER AT A COVERT TRAINING CAMP IN EASTERN CUBA.

THEIR MISSION WAS STILL UNDISCLOSED.

EVEN ITS LEADER WAS UNKNOWN...

...UNTIL A STRANGE MIDDLE-AGED MAN WITH A BALD PATE AND WEARING CIVILIAN CLOTHES ANNOUNCED...

CHE'S DISGUISE HAD WORKED. HIS PUFFY FACE, THE UPROOTING OF SOME HAIR, HIS OLDER APPEARANCE, ALL KEPT HIS IDENTITY A SECRET.

MY NAME IS RAMÓN, AND I WILL BE YOUR LEADER.

MEANWHILE, THE BOLIVIAN COMMUNIST LEADER MARIO MONJE HAD BEEN ORDERED BY CASTRO TO FIND AND BUY A TRAINING AREA IN BOLIVIA FOR CHE'S GUERRILLAS.

I WILL TAKE IT.

HE DID. A 3,700-ACRE PARCEL IN THE SOUTHEAST REGION OF THE COUNTRY.

97

ON NOVEMBER 3, 1966, CHE, POSING AS URUGUAYAN BUSINESSMAN ADOLFO MENA GONZÁLEZ AND SUPPOSEDLY WORKING FOR THE ORGANIZATION OF AMERICAN STATES, ARRIVED AT THE LUXURIOUS HOTEL COPACABANA IN LA PAZ, BOLIVIA'S LARGEST CITY.

TWO DAYS LATER, ACCOMPANIED BY FIVE COMPATRIOTS, HE BEGAN A THREE-DAY CROSSING OF THE COUNTRY TO THEIR BASE IN NANCAHUAZU.

CHE IS REPORTED TO HAVE OMINOUSLY TOLD ONE OF THESE COMRADES, THE BOLIVIAN COMMUNIST LORO VAZQUEZ-VIANA...

"I'VE COME TO STAY, AND THE ONLY WAY I WILL LEAVE HERE IS DEAD OR CROSSING A BORDER SHOOTING BULLETS AS I GO."

THE SMALL GUERRILLA FORCE NUMBERED ONLY 9 BOLIVIANS AND 24 MEN IN ALL.

98

AWAITING THE ARRIVAL OF MARIO MONJE MOLINA, WHO CHE HOPED WOULD DELIVER AT LEAST 20 BOLIVIAN GUERRILLAS, CHE TOLD HIS COMRADES...

WE HAVE TO CREATE ANOTHER VIETNAM IN THE AMERICAS, WITH ITS CENTER IN BOLIVIA.

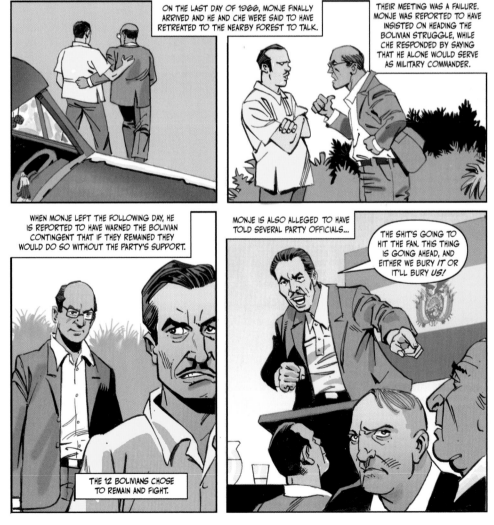

ON THE LAST DAY OF 1966, MONJE FINALLY ARRIVED AND HE AND CHE WERE SAID TO HAVE RETREATED TO THE NEARBY FOREST TO TALK.

THEIR MEETING WAS A FAILURE. MONJE WAS REPORTED TO HAVE INSISTED ON HEADING THE BOLIVIAN STRUGGLE, WHILE CHE RESPONDED BY SAYING THAT HE ALONE WOULD SERVE AS MILITARY COMMANDER.

WHEN MONJE LEFT THE FOLLOWING DAY, HE IS REPORTED TO HAVE WARNED THE BOLIVIAN CONTINGENT THAT IF THEY REMAINED THEY WOULD DO SO WITHOUT THE PARTY'S SUPPORT.

THE 12 BOLIVIANS CHOSE TO REMAIN AND FIGHT.

MONJE IS ALSO ALLEGED TO HAVE TOLD SEVERAL PARTY OFFICIALS...

THE SHIT'S GOING TO HIT THE FAN. THIS THING IS GOING AHEAD, AND EITHER WE BURY *IT* OR IT'LL BURY *US!*

99

FOR MUCH OF THE NEXT MONTH, CHE ATTEMPTED TO DISCIPLINE THE GUERRILLAS AND NORMALIZE THEIR BEHAVIOR SO NEARBY NEIGHBORS WOULDN'T BECOME SUSPICIOUS.

ON FEBRUARY 1, 1967, CHE LED MOST OF HIS CONTINGENT ON A TWO-WEEK TRAINING EXPEDITION INTO THE SURROUNDING WILDERNESS.

THEY SUFFERED HORRENDOUS STORMS, GOT LOST, AND RAN SHORT OF FOOD.

TWO OF THEM DROWNED.

THEY DID NOT RETURN UNTIL THE MIDDLE OF MARCH.

WHERE HAVE YOU *BEEN?*

IN A *NIGHTMARE.*

A BIGGER NIGHTMARE AWAITED THEM AT CAMP.

A GROUP OF NEW VOLUNTEERS HAD DESERTED, THE BOLIVIAN ARMY HAD CAPTURED ONE OF THEIR MESSENGERS, AND A SMALL AIRCRAFT HAD BEEN PATROLLING THE AREA FOR THE PAST THREE DAYS.

HOW ARE WE GOING TO BRING IN FOOD?

ALMOST IMMEDIATELY, THE REBEL GROUP WAS DISCOVERED AND THE ACCESS ROADS TO ITS CAMP WERE BLOCKED.

SOMETHING ELSE--OUR RADIO TRANSMITTER ISN'T WORKING.

FORTUNATELY, A DETACHMENT OF GUERRILLAS AMBUSHED A BOLIVIAN ARMY CONTINGENT ON MARCH 23, KILLING 7 AND CAPTURING 21 PRISONERS, AS WELL AS A LARGE HAUL OF MUNITIONS.

BUT DAYS LATER, GUERRILLA SCOUTS SPOTTED SOLDIERS IN SEVERAL PLACES NEARBY, AS WELL AS A LARGE CONTINGENT WITH A HELICOPTER AT THEIR CLOSEST NEIGHBORS DOWN THE MOUNTAINSIDE.

THE BOLIVIAN GOVERNMENT QUICKLY REPORTED THE EXISTENCE OF A GUERRILLA OPERATION, WHILE MAKING EXAGGERATED CLAIMS OF HAVING KILLED OR CAPTURED A LARGE CONTINGENT. CHE CONCLUDED...

OBVIOUSLY, THE DESERTERS OR THE PRISONERS TALKED. BUT WE DO NOT KNOW HOW MUCH THEY TOLD.

ENOUGH, HOWEVER, WAS LEARNED FOR BOLIVIAN PRESIDENT RENÉ BARRIENTOS TO CALL FOR CHE'S HEAD TO BE MOUNTED ON A PIKE IN LA PAZ, AND TO DECLARE THE GUERRILLAS SERVANTS OF...

...CASTRO COMMUNISM!

CHE AND HIS MEN HAD TO MOVE ON PREMATURELY IN ORDER TO FIND SAFETY FROM THE INCREASING NUMBER OF SOLDIERS SEARCHING FOR THEM.

IN EARLY APRIL, THE GUERRILLAS DID MANAGE TO AMBUSH AN ENEMY CONTINGENT.

"THERE WERE SEVEN DEAD, FIVE WOUNDED, AND 22 PRISONERS," CHE CLAIMED.

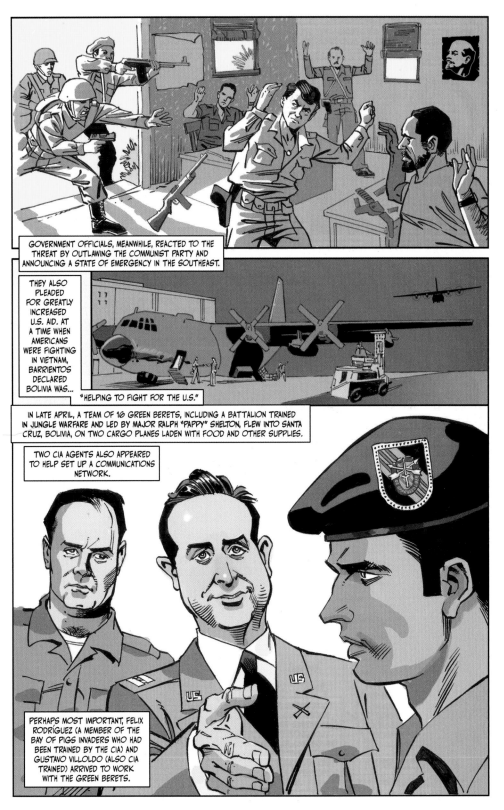

GOVERNMENT OFFICIALS, MEANWHILE, REACTED TO THE THREAT BY OUTLAWING THE COMMUNIST PARTY AND ANNOUNCING A STATE OF EMERGENCY IN THE SOUTHEAST.

THEY ALSO PLEADED FOR GREATLY INCREASED U.S. AID. AT A TIME WHEN AMERICANS WERE FIGHTING IN VIETNAM, BARRIENTOS DECLARED BOLIVIA WAS...

"HELPING TO FIGHT FOR THE U.S."

IN LATE APRIL, A TEAM OF 16 GREEN BERETS, INCLUDING A BATTALION TRAINED IN JUNGLE WARFARE AND LED BY MAJOR RALPH "PAPPY" SHELTON, FLEW INTO SANTA CRUZ, BOLIVIA, ON TWO CARGO PLANES LADEN WITH FOOD AND OTHER SUPPLIES.

TWO CIA AGENTS ALSO APPEARED TO HELP SET UP A COMMUNICATIONS NETWORK.

PERHAPS MOST IMPORTANT, FELIX RODRÍGUEZ (A MEMBER OF THE BAY OF PIGS INVADERS WHO HAD BEEN TRAINED BY THE CIA) AND GUSTAVO VILLOLDO (ALSO CIA TRAINED) ARRIVED TO WORK WITH THE GREEN BERETS.

CHE'S FORCES HAD FALLEN INTO A PAINFUL SURVIVAL MODE BY THE END OF APRIL. AS HE WROTE IN HIS DIARY...

NO RADIO CONTACT, NO HELP FROM BOLIVIANS.

AND MY ASTHMA GETS WORSE AND WORSE IN THIS DAMN JUNGLE.

"...ISOLATION APPEARS TO BE COMPLETE, SICKNESSES HAVE UNDERMINED THE HEALTH OF SOME COMRADES, FORCING US TO DIVIDE FORCES...AS YET WE HAVE BEEN UNABLE TO ESTABLISH CONTACT WITH JOAQUIN...NOT ONE ENLISTMENT HAS BEEN OBTAINED."

BUT WE'VE GOT TO GO ON!

TUMA! TUMA! HANG ON! PLEASE!

THIS "BATTLE AGAINST IMPERIALISM" AND "AGAINST THE GREAT ENEMY OF MANKIND: THE UNITED STATES OF AMERICA," AS CHE HAD WRITTEN, JUST MIGHT NOT SUCCEED.

CHE SOON LEARNED THAT A SEPARATE COLUMN OF HIS MEN HAD BEEN MASSACRED IN AN AMBUSH...

...THAT DESTROYED PERHAPS A THIRD OF HIS ENTIRE FORCE.

IN EARLY OCTOBER, CHE'S GUERRILLAS, WHICH NOW CONSISTED OF A SCANT 17 MEN, WERE HUNGRY AND BEATEN AS THEY MARCHED DOWNHILL FROM THEIR MOUNTAIN RETREAT.

A NEWLY SCHOOLED UNIT OF BOLIVIAN RANGERS, INFORMED OF THE REBELS' WHEREABOUTS, OPENED FIRE ON THEM.

CHE WAS WOUNDED IN HIS LEFT LEG.

HE AND A BOLIVIAN COMRADE TRIED TO ESCAPE, BUT...

DO NOT *SHOOT!* I AM CHE GUEVARA AND I AM WORTH MORE TO YOU ALIVE THAN DEAD!

CHE SUPPOSEDLY SAID.

MINUTES LATER, THE UNIT'S CAPTAIN IDENTIFIED CHE, AND TIED HIM WITH HIS OWN BELT.

THAT EVENING, HIS HANDS AND FEET TIED, CHE WAS PLACED WITH TWO DEAD COMRADES ON THE DIRT FLOOR OF A DILAPIDATED SCHOOLHOUSE IN THE DESOLATE VILLAGE OF LA HIGUERA. THERE HE WAS QUESTIONED BY LIEUTENANT COLONEL ANDRÉS SELICH.

I FIND YOU SOMEWHAT DEPRESSED. CAN YOU EXPLAIN WHY I GET THIS IMPRESSION?

I'VE FAILED. IT'S ALL OVER.

WHAT MADE YOU DECIDE TO OPERATE IN OUR COUNTRY?

CAN'T YOU SEE THE STATE IN WHICH THE PEASANTS LIVE?

THEY'RE ALMOST LIKE *SAVAGES*, LIVING IN A STATE OF POVERTY THAT DEPRESSES THE HEART.

BY THE TIME CIA AGENT FELIX RODRÍGUEZ ARRIVED THE FOLLOWING MORNING AND TRIED TO QUESTION CHE...

...CHE HAD NOTHING MORE TO SAY.

THERE HAVE BEEN MANY VERSIONS OF CHE'S EXECUTION. THE FOLLOWING SEEMS THE MOST LIKELY: A DIRECTIVE HAD COME IN, PRESUMABLY FROM PRESIDENT BARRIENTOS.

WE ARE TO KILL THIS GUEVARA IMMEDIATELY.

A GROUP OF SOLDIERS DREW STRAWS TO DETERMINE WHO WOULD RECEIVE THE HONOR OF CARRYING OUT THE ORDER.

IT IS MY LUCKY DAY.

SERGEANT MARIO TERÁN DREW THE WINNING SHORT STRAW.

FELIX RODRÍGUEZ SUPPOSEDLY INSTRUCTED TERÁN TO AIM CAREFULLY AND MAKE IT APPEAR THAT CHE HAD BEEN KILLED IN ACTION AND NOT BY EXECUTION.

BEFORE BEING SHOT, CHE ALLEGEDLY TOLD TERÁN...

THEN THE DEED WAS DONE.

I KNOW YOU ARE HERE TO KILL ME. *SHOOT*, COWARD, YOU ARE ONLY GOING TO KILL A MAN.

IT WAS OCTOBER 9, 1967. CHE GUEVARA WAS DEAD AT THE AGE OF 39.

YEARS LATER, CHE'S REMAINS WERE BROUGHT TO CUBA. ON OCTOBER 17, 1997, THEY WERE LAID TO REST WITH FULL HONORS IN A NEWLY CONSTRUCTED MAUSOLEUM IN THE CITY OF SANTA CLARA, THE SCENE OF ONE OF HIS MOST DECISIVE BATTLES.

DURING HIS LIFE AND PERHAPS MORE SINCE HIS DEATH, CHE GUEVARA HAS ELICITED CONTROVERSY AND DIVERSE OPINIONS OF WHAT HE WAS AND WHAT HE REPRESENTED. HERE ARE JUST A FEW...

"WITHOUT TRIAL HE WAS DECLARED A MURDERER, STOOD AGAINST A WALL AND SHOT. HISTORICALLY SPEAKING, JUSTICE HAS RARELY BEEN BETTER SERVED."
HUMBERTO FONTOVA, AUTHOR OF *EXPOSING THE REAL CHE GUEVARA*

"THOUGH COMMUNISM MAY HAVE LOST ITS FIRE, HE REMAINS THE POTENT SYMBOL OF REBELLION AND THE ALLURING ZEAL OF REVOLUTION."
ARIEL DORFMAN, CHILEAN NOVELIST, PLAYWRIGHT, ESSAYIST, HUMAN-RIGHTS ADVOCATE, AND PROFESSOR AT DUKE UNIVERSITY

"HE WAS A TOTALITARIAN. HE ACHIEVED NOTHING BUT DISASTER."
PAUL BERMAN, AUTHOR AND JOURNALIST, AND DISTINGUISHED WRITER IN RESIDENCE AT NEW YORK UNIVERSITY

"TODAY CHE'S IMAGE IS EVERYWHERE IN BOLIVIA, AND HE IS PARTICULARLY ESTEEMED BY THAT COUNTRY'S MOST POWERFUL PEASANT AND INDIGENOUS MOVEMENT."
HISTORIAN AND AUTHOR GREG GRANDIN, WHO ALSO TEACHES AT NEW YORK UNIVERSITY

"NOW WE ALL KNOW THE GOOD THINGS ABOUT CHE, BUT LET'S LOOK AT A COUPLE OF PROBLEMS: THE NEW MAN HAD NO ROOM FOR THE NEW GAY MAN AND, BESIDES THAT, CHE CONTRIBUTED TO THE SILENCING OF CRITICS OF THE REVOLUTION.
AND IF ONE THING UNDERMINES REVOLUTIONARY GAINS IT IS THE UNWILLINGNESS TO LISTEN TO INTERNAL CRITICISM."
JEFF BROWITT, AUTHOR AND SENIOR LECTURER IN LATIN AMERICAN STUDIES AT THE UNIVERSITY OF TECHNOLOGY, SYDNEY

"WHAT DOES GUEVARA'S MEMORY OFFER THE WORLD TODAY? PERHAPS PRIMARILY HIS PERSONAL EXAMPLE, HIS ARTHURIAN QUALITIES, THAT REMARKABLE DETERMINATION TO STRUGGLE AND SACRIFICE FOR A SET OF BELIEFS."
HENRY BUTTERFIELD RYAN, RETIRED U.S. FOREIGN-SERVICE OFFICER AND AUTHOR OF *THE FALL OF CHE GUEVARA*

Chronology of a Revolutionary

JUNE 14, 1928--ERNESTO GUEVARA DE
LA SERNA BORN IN ROSARIO, ARGENTINA.

1947--GUEVARA FAMILY MOVES TO BUENOS
AIRES; ERNESTO STARTS MEDICAL SCHOOL.

1950--ERNESTO TRAVELS BY MOTORBIKE
THROUGH NORTHERN ARGENTINA.

1952--ERNESTO TRAVELS THROUGH LATIN
AMERICA WITH ALBERTO GRANADO.

1953--ERNESTO GRADUATES FROM MEDICAL
SCHOOL, VISITS BOLIVIA AND OTHER COUNTRIES.

JULY 10, 1955--ERNESTO MEETS FIDEL CASTRO
IN MEXICO CITY AND JOINS JULY 26 MOVEMENT.

NOVEMBER 25, 1956--ERNESTO SAILS WITH
CASTRO ON THE *GRANMA* IN INVASION OF CUBA.

1958--ERNESTO, NOW ALREADY CHE, LEADS
CAPTURE OF SANTA CLARA.

1959--CHE APPOINTED COMMANDER OF LA
CABANA FORTRESS, THEN PRESIDENT OF
THE BANK OF CUBA.

APRIL 17-20, 1961--BAY OF PIGS INVASION FAILS.

APRIL 24, 1965--CHE ARRIVES IN CONGO TO BEGIN
GUERRILLA OPERATIONS.

1966--CHE LIVES SECETLY IN DAR ES SALAAM,
THEN PRAGUE, AND BRIEFLY IN CUBA.

NOVEMBER 3, 1966--CHE ARRIVES IN BOLIVIA.

APRIL 17, 1967--CHE DIVIDES GUERRILLAS AND CAN
NEVER RELOCATE A GROUP LED BY JOAQUIN.

APRIL 29, 1967--GREEN BERETS ARRIVE TO TRAIN BOLIVIANS.

AUGUST 6, 1967--BOLIVIAN SOLDIERS UNCOVER GUERRILLA
EQUIPMENT AND DOCUMENTS, ESTABLISH CHE'S PRESENCE.

OCTOBER 8, 1967--
A WOUNDED CHE
IS CAPTURED.

OCTOBER 9, 1967--CHE IS EXECUTED BY THE BOLIVIANS.

OCTOBER 15, 1967--CASTRO DECLARES THREE DAYS OF
MOURNING AND PROCLAIMS OCTOBER 8 AN ANNUAL
HOLIDAY IN CHE'S HONOR.

HASTA
LA VICTORIA
SIEMPRE

JULY 4, 1997--CHE'S SKELETON IS FOUND IN BOLIVIA AND
SENT TO CUBA, WHERE IT IS INTERRED AT SANTA CLARA.

ACKNOWLEDGMENTS

WE HAPPILY ACKNOWLEDGE OUR EDITOR AND PUBLISHER, THOMAS LEBIEN, FOR HIS WISE AND PERCEPTIVE EDITING, HIS ENDLESS PATIENCE, AND HIS CONSTANT FRIENDSHIP; ELIZABETH MAPLES FOR HER NECESSARY AND UNWAVERING ASSISTANCE IN SO MANY THINGS; AND JOE RUBENSTEIN FOR HIS SUPERB AND MUCH APPRECIATED AID WITH THE INKING.